THE LEGEND OF

RITCHIE BROS.
AUCTIONEERS

SECOND EDITION

THE LEGEND OF

RITCHIE BROS.
AUCTIONEERS

JEFFREY L. RODENGEN

Edited by Jon VanZile
Design and layout by Joey Henderson and Wendy Iverson

For Jean-Pierre,
whose final bid wins all our hearts.

WRITE STUFF

Write Stuff Enterprises, Inc.
1001 South Andrews Avenue
Second Floor
Fort Lauderdale, FL 33316
1-800-900-Book (1-800-900-2665)
(954) 462-6657
www.writestuffbooks.com

Publisher's Cataloging in Publication

Rodengen, Jeffrey L.
    The legend of Ritchie Bros. Auctioneers/
Jeffrey L. Rodengen. – 2nd ed.
    p. cm.
    Includes bibliographical references and index.
    ISBN 0-945903-59-6
    1. Ritchie Bros. Auctioneers, Inc. – History.
2. Auctioneers – United States. 3. Industrial
equipment industry agents – United States.
I. Title.

HF5477.U64R58 2000   381.17'065
                                QBI99-1603

Library of Congress
Catalog Card Number 99-096783

ISBN 0-945903-59-6

Completely produced in the
United States of America
10 9 8 7 6 5 4 3 2 1

Also by Jeffrey L. Rodengen

The Legend of Chris-Craft

IRON FIST:
The Lives of Carl Kiekhaefer

Evinrude-Johnson and
The Legend of OMC

Serving the Silent Service:
The Legend of Electric Boat

The Legend of
Dr Pepper/Seven-Up

The Legend of Honeywell

The Legend of Briggs & Stratton

The Legend of Ingersoll-Rand

The Legend of Stanley:
150 Years of The Stanley Works

The MicroAge Way

The Legend of Halliburton

The Legend of York International

The Legend of Nucor Corporation

The Legend of Goodyear:
The First 100 Years

The Legend of AMP

The Legend of Cessna

The Legend of VF Corporation

The Spirit of AMD

The Legend of Rowan

New Horizons:
The Story of Ashland Inc.

The History of American Standard

The Legend of Mercury Marine

The Legend of Federal-Mogul

Against the Odds:
Inter-Tel—The First 30 Years

The Legend of Pfizer

State of the Heart:
The Practical Guide to Your Heart
and Heart Surgery
with Larry W. Stephenson, M.D.

The Legend of
Worthington Industries

The Legend of IBP, Inc.

The Legend of
Trinity Industries, Inc.

The Legend of
Cornelius Vanderbilt Whitney

The Legend of Amdahl

The Legend of Litton Industries

The Legend of Gulfstream

The Legend of Bertram
with David A. Patten

The Legend of ALLTEL
with David A. Patten

The Yes, you can of
Invacare Corporation
with Anthony L. Wall

The Ship in the Balloon:
The Story of Boston Scientific
and the Development of
Less-Invasive Medicine

The Legend of
Day & Zimmermann

The Legend of Noble Drilling

Fifty Years of Innovation:
Kulicke & Soffa

Biomet—From Warsaw
to the World
with Richard F. Hubbard

NRA: An American Legend

The Heritage and Values
of RPM, Inc.

The Marmon Group:
The First Fifty Years

The Legend of Grainger

The Legend of
The Titan Corporation
with Richard F. Hubbard

The Legend of Discount Tire Co.
with Richard F. Hubbard

The Legend of Polaris
with Richard F. Hubbard

The Legend of La-Z-Boy
with Richard F. Hubbard

The Legend of McCarthy
with Richard F. Hubbard

InterVoice:
Twenty Years of Innovation
with Richard F. Hubbard

Jefferson-Pilot Financial:
A Century of Excellence
with Richard F. Hubbard

The Legend of HCA
with Richard F. Hubbard

The Legend of Werner Enterprises
with Richard F. Hubbard

The Legend of J. F. Shea Co.
with Richard F. Hubbard

TABLE OF CONTENTS

INTRODUCTION

THERE IS NO OTHER company in the world quite like Ritchie Bros. Auctioneers. By far the world's largest auctioneer of industrial and heavy equipment, Ritchie Bros. has sold billions upon billions of dollars of used heavy equipment over the last three decades. The Vancouver company has hosted auctions in places as varied as the high Canadian Rockies and the windblown deserts of Dubai.

According to most analysts and industry observers, Ritchie Bros. almost single-handedly deserves credit for bringing legitimacy and consolidation to the global used industrial equipment auctioneering business. And according to the many customers and consignors who regularly use Ritchie Bros.' services, the company's hospitality, integrity, and work ethic are unmatched.

This kind of praise is remarkable considering even the recent history of used-equipment auctions. Until the 1960s, equipment auctions were generally viewed with suspicion. They were seen as events that were rigged for the equipment owners. Buybacks, in which owners bid up the prices of their own equipment, were common, and auctioneers were sometimes known to take the entire proceeds of a sale—often the result of a lifetime's hard work for a contractor—and disappear. Ritchie Bros. Auctioneers is the company that changed all this.

The story begins in western Canada's fertile Okanagan Valley. That's where Rae George Ritchie settled with his wife, Ruby Beryl, after World War I. The couple had four boys: Bill, who was killed in World War II during D-Day, Ken, John, and Dave, and two daughters, Ellen and Margaret. To support his family, Rae George ran a stamp and coin shop and furniture store. The Ritchie children worked in the store, buying and selling secondhand furniture and honing their "second hand sense," or nose for a good deal.

As they grew up, Ken, John, and Dave slowly took over the family business and began expanding it. First they added a sporting-goods shop—from which they liberally borrowed fishing and hockey gear—and later an auction business.

The auction company, however, was born more of necessity than from any organized business plan. In 1958, when the Royal Bank suddenly called in a $2,000 payment on a $10,000 loan, the Ritchie boys found themselves in desperate need of quick cash. To raise it, they raced to arrange an auction at the old Scout Hall in Kelowna. The sale was a success, and the seeds of an idea began to germinate.

Before long, the trio of rowdy young men—avid hunters and fishermen, skiers and lacrosse players—began combing the countryside looking for more goods to auction. They sold off sawmills and depleted mining operations, machine shops, and even entire towns. Gradually, they reached beyond the lush Okanagan for ever larger spreads of equipment.

At this point, with their business performing well in a relatively small universe, the three Ritchie brothers had a decision to make. They could remain in the Okanagan indefinitely with a smallish and respectable auction company, or they could gamble and push south into the United States and perhaps someday across the world. Dave Ritchie, the youngest of the three, favored rapid expansion and moved his family to Vancouver in the early 1960s to set up the company's first satellite office.

From there, the company did indeed move into fertile auction grounds in the United States, throughout Canada, and across all of North America. There was plenty of competition, but Ritchie Bros.' strength lay in the people running it. Dave Ritchie, assuming a greater role as his brothers gradually phased themselves out of the growing business, was absolutely inflexible in his principles. At Ritchie Bros. auctions, consignors were offered guaranteed minimum auction proceeds for their equipment spreads, a practice unheard of at the time, and owner bid-ins or buybacks were completely forbidden.

And, as Ritchie Bros. was earning a reputation for integrity, word spread throughout the auction industry that Ritchie Bros.' auctions were also an awful lot of fun. The company sponsored extravagant parties before or after sales. Key customers were taken fishing or on weekend trips to hunting lodges and game camps.

The auctions themselves were entertaining, and while hundreds of thousands of dollars in used equipment rumbled across Ritchie Bros.' trademark ramp, spectators sat amid the lyrical ebb and flow of the auctioneer's song and the smell of frying hamburgers and onions. It was, as one long-time supporter described, "part P.T. Barnum."

By the 1980s and 1990s, Ritchie Bros. was ready to launch from North America into the rest of the world, conducting auctions and opening yards in Europe, the Pacific, Asia, the Middle East, and anywhere else there was a need for an honest auctioneering company.

Ritchie Bros.' years of rapid and global growth are studded with incredible stories and historically important sales. From auctioning equipment used in the *Exxon Valdez* oil spill cleanup to selling off material from the Falkland Islands war, Ritchie Bros. is often the company called in to clean up history's stage.

Today, with annual sales of more than $1 billion, Ritchie Bros. Auctioneers is by far the largest industrial equipment auction company in the world. Still run by Dave Ritchie and a tight cadre of veterans, including Russ Cmolik and others, the company has maintained the bedrock principles that were first articulated decades ago by a trio of ambitious young men. Yet the Ritchie Bros. of 2004 is a thoroughly modern creation. Using money from a 1998 public offering on the New York Stock Exchange, Ritchie Bros. engineered the 1999 acquisition of its largest competitor. The company is also keeping a watchful eye on developing technology and leading its industry in careful application of this technology to auctioneering.

This forward-thinking application of new ideas balanced against time-honored principles has earned Ritchie Bros. Auctioneers the preeminent place in the global $100 billion used-equipment industry.

ACKNOWLEDGMENTS

RESEARCHING AND WRITing *The Legend of Ritchie Bros. Auctioneers* would not have been possible without the assistance of a great many people.

Bill Kimmet, my research assistant in Vancouver, helped compile the archival research and compose the first narrative timeline.

The Ritchie brothers themselves, and other senior management of the company, also provided invaluable assistance through the generous donation of their time and their memories. Dave Ritchie, CEO and chairman of Ritchie Bros. Auctioneers, provided hours of interviews in addition to artwork that lends content and texture to this remarkable story. Similarly, Ken and John Ritchie contributed anecdotes from the company's earliest days that provide flavor and depth.

Company President Russ Cmolik provided his own excellent memory and stories, and his guidance is deeply appreciated.

This book also would not have been possible without the patient assistance of Season Johnson, marketing coordinator, and Hanna de Guzman, former marketing coordinator. Working closely with Write Stuff staff, Johnson provided a vital link between Ritchie Bros. offices and the Write Stuff team of editors and artists.

As with any oral history, the information compiled during hundreds of hours of interviews was crucial. The author wishes to thank the Ritchie Bros. employees, present and former, and many faithful customers who participated in the project.

This extensive list includes Dennis Armstrong, territory manager, Ritchie Bros. Auctioneers; Ed Banser, south central vice president, Ritchie Bros. Auctioneers; Dick Bartel, retired president, Ritchie Bros. Auctioneers; Bill Bennett, former premier of British Columbia; Peter Blake, chief financial officer, Ritchie Bros. Auctioneers; Bob Brawley, vice president, Ritchie Bros. Auctioneers; Bill Bremmeyer, owner of Bremmeyer Logging Company in Washington state; Matt Campbell, president and CEO, Hammer Equipment Sales Ltd.; Bob Carswell, senior valuation analyst, Ritchie Bros. Auctioneers; Gary Caufield, former corporate controller and currently in the title division, Ritchie Bros. Auctioneers; Don Chalmers, vice president Western Canada, Ritchie Bros. Auctioneers; Malcolm Clay, partner with the accounting firm of KPMG, LLP; Rick Hullett,

Ritchie Bros. customer; Dave Husby, president, Husby Forest Products; John Ivester, former owner of *The Last Bid*; Dave Kruse with Peter Kiewit Sons Inc.; Frank McFadden, senior valuation analyst, Ritchie Bros. Auctioneers; Bill Miller, former owner of Miller and Miller; Marty Pope, vice president, Ritchie Bros. Auctioneers; John Reid, Ritchie Bros. customer; Randy Ringhaver, president, Ring Power Corporation; Tammy Ritchie, manager of the Stuart Island fishing camp and Dave Ritchie's daughter; Roger Rummel, vice president, Ritchie Bros. Auctioneers; Roland Russell, president, El-Russ Equipment; Terry Simpson, Ritchie Bros. customer; Clay Tippett, marketing manager, Ritchie Bros. Auctioneers; Sylvain Touchette, vice president, Ritchie Bros. Auctioneers; Peter Van Vreumingen, former accountant, Ritchie Bros. Auctioneers; and John Wild, employee, Ritchie Bros. Auctioneers.

Finally, a special word of thanks to the staff at Write Stuff. Proofreader Bonnie Freeman, transcriptionist Mary Aaron, and indexer Erica Orloff worked quickly and efficiently. Particular thanks also go to Jon VanZile, executive editor; Melody Maysonet and Heather G. Cohn, associate editors; Amanda Fowler and Nancy Rackear, executive assistants; Sandy Cruz, senior art director; Dennis Shockley, Joey Henderson, Rachelle Donley, and Wendy Iverson, art directors; Fred Moll and Bruce Borich, production managers; Marianne Roberts, office manager; Grace Kurotori, director of trade shows and promotions; Rory Schmer, distribution supervisor; and Karine Rodengen, project coordinator.

The Ritchie family store, with its trademark "BUY, SELL or TRADE" sign, pictured in 1946. At the time this picture was taken, Rae George Ritchie had bought a half interest in the O.K. Used Furniture Store in the same building.

CHAPTER ONE

THAT SECONDHAND SENSE

THE BEGINNING—1960

We've come a long way from the old Scout Hall in Kelowna, where we
held our first auction in order to pay down $2,000 on a bank loan.

—Dave Ritchie, 1998

STORIES ABOUND ABOUT THE early days of Ritchie Bros. Auctioneers—and most of them are probably true. There was the time that brother John Ritchie decorated the front window of the family furniture store with a hammerhead shark that he passed off as the legendary Ogopogo creature from nearby Lake Okanagan. Soon, busloads of children were coming to see the mythical Canadian equivalent of the Loch Ness monster.

Or when the brothers hired locals to picket their own store, paying them a dollar an hour to carry signs that read "Prices in This Store Are Too Low" so passersby would think the competition was protesting.

Or the ceaseless practical jokes on each other and everyone else, like the time Dave Ritchie bought a painting of a man swimming nude in a pool. Dave had heard that one of his customers had just bought a pool that he loved, so Dave, being a kind and gracious host, decided to present his customer with this "commissioned piece of art" at a big party with the customer's friends and colleagues. In front of everybody, the man watched in indignant horror as the painting was unveiled and everyone hooted and clapped. The next day,

after the gag was revealed and his friend had calmed down, Dave offered the painting at auction.

And the parties. They were standard fare at any Ritchie Bros. sale. Even when the company had taken a rare beating at an unsuccessful sale, the brothers would still spring for steaks, music, and plenty of beer, hosting a party for their customers that might last until sunrise, when all the partners and Ritchie Bros. employees realized they had to go back to work. Yet they always did go back to work because the work ethic of the company was never allowed to suffer.

Fishing turned out to be another important building block of the auction house. From the beginning, the avid sportsmen took customers and friends (usually one and the same) up into mountain lakes or out salmon fishing on the cold swells of the North Pacific. Their business attracted a certain breed of customer. He was usually a self-made entrepreneur and contractor

Pictured at age 24, Dave Ritchie poses with the family delivery truck. During high school, all of the Ritchie boys worked in the store, where they learned to deal in used goods.

12   THE LEGEND OF RITCHIE BROS. AUCTIONEERS

who was savvy, smart, down-to-earth, and hard working.

And he wasn't afraid to risk a little of his fortune in a friendly game of cards. They would gather in hunting and fishing lodges at night for poker and blackjack games. In the big games, sometimes more money would change hands across the table than had during that day's auction.

But this was how the brothers, Ken, John, and Dave Ritchie, built their business from nothing into a billion-dollar global industrial auction powerhouse. There is no other company in the world exactly like Ritchie Bros. Auctioneers, none that has been able to match the balance of principled hard work, riotous good times, and an all-consuming loyalty to the customer. Few companies have come to symbolize their industry in the way that Ritchie Bros. Auctioneers, led by Dave Ritchie, has become synonymous with the global business of industrial equipment auctioneering.

Left: Ruby Beryl Staples, who married Rae George Ritchie in 1924. Relatively new to Kelowna at the time, the Stapleses came from Manitoba, where they had been successful farmers.

Below: The Ritchie men posing together, most likely in the late 1950s or early 1960s. From left to right: John, Rae George, Ken, and Dave Ritchie.

80 thousand, OK I'll do 75, 75, 75, now 80, 80, now 85, 85, 85 and 90, 90 thousand, 90, 90, 90. Dave, does your man want one

CHAPTER ONE: THAT SECONDHAND SENSE   13

Grandpa George

The story begins with a young adventurer of British descent named George Ritchie, the boys' paternal grandfather. George Ritchie wandered north to the goldfields of British Columbia and the town of Barkerville in the Cariboo area in the 1880s. Barkerville, the largest boomtown west of Chicago and north of San Francisco, had been founded in 1862 when Welshman Billy Barker discovered gold deposits and touched off a gold rush.

From Barkerville, George Ritchie traveled south to Vancouver, passing through Kelowna, the town that would become home to the Ritchie family. Dave Ritchie later described his grandfather's trip: "He left there and decided to walk to Vancouver through the Okanagan, a fertile, fruit-growing valley in central British Columbia, and that is when he first saw the town of Kelowna."[1]

George didn't stop in the picturesque little town that day. Instead, he kept walking and soon arrived in Vancouver, where he purchased a house for $400. At the time he arrived, Vancouver was a rapidly growing city on the balmy Pacific shore of southern British Columbia. Sensing an opportunity, George became a building contractor and joined in the aggressive building boom.

In 1891, George got married, and in 1894, he and his wife welcomed a son, Rae George Ritchie. The couple would ultimately have four children: Rae George, Ralph, Tom, and Hazel.

Rae George was an independent child from a very young age. When he was just 11, he left home to work in a local dairy, where he saved his money to buy a tea set for his mother. (The set remained in the family for decades.) In 1914, at the age of 19, Rae George volunteered to serve in the Canadian army during World War I. He participated in Vimy Ridge, a historic and hard-fought battle that defined a generation of Canadians and was an important element in the Allied victory.

When he returned to Canada, Rae George entered McGill University—a renowned school in Montreal—determined to study law. While at school, he was awarded the Governor General's Award for Excellence. He graduated and moved to Kelowna, a small town located in the heart of the British Columbia orchard belt, and set up a law practice. Around the same time, George Ritchie moved with his son Ralph to California, where he remained in the construction business until his death in 1939.

A Ritchie Family War Hero

Around the same time Rae George emigrated to Kelowna, the Staples family moved into town. An accomplished farming family, the Stapleses relocated from Manitoba to a farm on Bernard Avenue, which would later become one of Kelowna's main streets. Within a few years of the move, Ruby Beryl Staples and Rae George Ritchie were courting. In 1924, they married and before long had the first of their six children, a son named Bill. He was followed by Ken, Ellen, twins John and Margaret, and Dave, who was born in 1936.

Unfortunately, war would once again interrupt Rae George's life. When World War II broke out and Canada entered the conflict, the two eldest Ritchie men, Rae George and Bill, reported for duty. Again the Canadian forces, numbering one million by the end of the conflict, played an important part in the Allied effort. Canada was assigned one of the five beaches in the heroic D-day invasion. Bill Ritchie, the oldest son, was killed in action during the invasion.

After the war, Rae George, who had served out his hitch in Canada, once again returned to Kelowna. This time, however, he had lost his oldest son and came back angry and heartbroken. "He always said that he had been born too young for the first war and too old for the second," later remarked Tammy Ritchie, Rae George's granddaughter.[2]

As compensation for loss, the Ritchie family was awarded a monthly War Service Gratuity for the amount of $668.87 in the name of Bill Ritchie. Decades later, in 1999, Canada would honor Bill Ritchie by naming a mountain lake in his memory.[3]

Above: A luggage display in the Ritchie family store, pictured in 1946. The family business gradually expanded from a stamp and coin shop into used furniture, luggage, and finally sporting goods.

Below: The Ritchie brothers were avid lacrosse players, and many who knew them as boys remembered their competitiveness and relentless practice. Ken Ritchie is the goalie (just behind the trophy), Dave is in the last row (fourth from right), and John is in the second (at far right).

When he got home, Rae George decided not to pursue law. Instead, he used Bill's war gratuity to invest in a stamp and coin business called the B.C. Stamp Exchange. He ran it from his Burne Avenue house, beginning trade in 1946. It wasn't a big business, but it grew well enough, and soon Rae George was sending stamps and coins to collectors throughout North America. Before long, he had grown his business enough to lease space in the front of the O.K. Used Furniture Store at 239 Bernard Avenue— much to the delight of his wife, who wanted "to get him out from under her feet."[4]

Even with the new space, the business was still small. Its new headquarters measured 17 feet by 50 feet, room enough for a desk and several safes filled with collectible stamps and coins.

At the end of the year, another opportunity presented itself. In late 1946, less than a year after Rae George moved into the building, one of the partners in the O.K. Used Furniture Store sold his half interest in the business to Rae George for $865. Every Saturday night from then on, the two remaining partners, Rae George and Mike Weiglittner, sat at the Ritchies' kitchen table and split the weekly revenue, leaving about

$50 in the till for the next week's business. This ritual lasted until 1949, when Weiglittner agreed to sell Rae George the remaining half of the business for $1,765.[5]

The Ritchie family now had its own business, and the kids were encouraged to participate. "I couldn't wait to get there after school," said Dave Ritchie, who was in his teens. "I wanted to see what we had bought or sold. It was the greatest learning experience that anyone could ever get, and all the kids worked in the store after school."[6]

By now, the large family was a fixture in Kelownan social life, and Rae George presided over his family with discipline and street smarts. Rae George himself was an interesting, stately, and even slightly intimidating figure in town. Fellow Kelownans remember seeing him ride the streets on his bicycle, wearing an impressive cowboy hat.

"I think there were influences in the Ritchie house that went beyond what a normal kid would find," remembered Bill Bennett, a family friend. "There was a lot of direction from their father that made them pretty streetwise. He taught them trading, and the business of trading is a great educator because you're dealing with all sorts of people and everything is a contest."[7] Bennett would later be elected premier of British Columbia.

Rae George ran the business until 1950, when his sons took it over. Five years later, after Dave graduated from high school, the brothers formed a partnership to buy the family store from their father. When the partnership was founded, Kelowna had about 5,500 residents.

Good Times Were Had by All

The 1950s were good to the Ritchie family. The business, now owned by the three boys, grew as the postwar economic boom spread across North America. The boys themselves were also growing up and taking advantage of all the natural assets that a place like Kelowna had to offer. Located as it was in rolling and fertile fruit country, the Okanagan Valley was blessed with sports activities, and Kelowna was a safe, small town where everybody knew everybody else. The Ritchie boys could walk across all of Kelowna or hitchhike up into the mountains to fish for trout. After a long day fishing, they'd walk home after dark—unless it was too dark; then they'd pitch a temporary camp in the bush and sleep under the stars.

"We'd go to Shannon Lake on the ferry," remembered Dave. "It was a nickel if you didn't have a ticket, but we would still run around the ferry in front of the ticket collector so we'd never have to pay the two-and-one-half-cent fare. Shannon Lake was the only lake in the Okanagan that had bass and perch in it. Then we'd hitchhike home."[8]

Salmon, too, were highly prized trophies. The brothers went out in the creeks after kokanee, or landlocked Pacific salmon. The sweet little fish would fetch 20 cents a dozen for females or 25 cents a dozen for the larger males. "We'd catch them after school and sell them," remembered Dave. "Of course, the game warden was always chasing us. It was almost Huckleberry Finn–type stuff, and it was a wonderful life."[9]

Besides fishing, the avid outdoorsmen hunted cougar, skied in the Canadian Rockies, boated, played hockey and baseball, and became accomplished lacrosse players. Bennett remembered that the Ritchie boys "attacked lacrosse and were well known for their abilities."[10]

They were also known for their rowdy sociability. They played hard, got into the occasional spot of trouble, hosted all-night poker games, sometimes fought among themselves, and earned the grounded sensibility of small-town traders and businessmen.

This play-hard/work-hard attitude was partially the influence of their father. From an early age, work was a constant in their lives. At times, Dave worked on the McFarlands' local farm, picking and selling asparagus and laboring as a roofer. One summer he took the money he had earned from roofing and bought a cabin at Island Lake.

number 1884. Does he want all three at that price? He takes them all! Of course he does! Three times the money.

16   THE LEGEND OF RITCHIE BROS. AUCTIONEERS

"One particular day, we were up there with two redbone cougar hounds called Jack and Dan," Dave said.

We always took them out fishing, and they'd be out in the bush running around, chasing everything they could. My mother had made a nice chicken for our dinner, and we just put the chicken on the table and went out fishing. Ken went one way and I went the other way. We both come back, and the chicken is gone. I thought he took it and he thought I took it, so we're both standing there pointing at each other. But it was old Jack. The dog had eaten up the whole chicken. Chicken bones aren't good for dogs, so he was moaning and groaning for quite a while.[11]

The brothers were an ambitious group and wanted to expand their family business; they soon settled on a natural choice. Sporting goods were added to the furniture. Of course, the boys themselves weren't above "borrowing" from their fishing tackle and often snagged the best plugs for themselves and their many friends.

In these early days, the boys' personalities began to emerge. Dave was the most intense of the three, a stubborn, friendly, generous, and aggressive competitor. Even though he was the youngest, Dave could handle himself well physically and gave as good as he got from his older brothers.

John, although shy as a young child, matured into a prankster extraordinaire. He had tremendous energy and a natural ability to get people to do what he wanted, convince them of almost anything, and come up with creative ways to advertise his family's business in an age before television. On one occasion, he tacked $1 bills throughout the store and invited customers to pick one and use it toward their purchase. People lined up outside.[12]

On another occasion, John parlayed a local legend into a small tourist trade. Nearby Lake Okanagan was supposedly home to the mythical Ogopogo, an aquatic throwback to the dinosaurs. John announced that the Chamber of Commerce had found a baby Ogopogo on the beach and displayed the creature in the front window of the store. Before long, tours of schoolchildren were coming by to look at it. (It was actually a hammerhead shark.)[13]

Ken, the eldest, was more serious than the other two, and many people remember his disposition as striking a middle ground between his two younger brothers' personalities.

Shortly after sporting goods were included, the brothers added luggage to the inventory and expanded the store by renting lots at 235 Bernard Avenue and 241 Bernard Avenue. The brothers next purchased the contents of the Old Curiosity Shop in Vancouver, adding antiques. The inventory from this store was shipped to Kelowna and sold.[14] Throughout the expansions, Rae George was content with the B.C. Stamp Exchange and left the other ventures to his sons.

A $2,000 Wake-Up Call

Things might have continued like this indefinitely and auctioneering might never have entered the picture were it not for a pivotal event in 1958. That year, the Royal Bank unexpectedly demanded a $2,000 payment on a $10,000 loan. The Ritchie family was unable to pay the amount on such short notice and didn't know what to do until a family friend made a suggestion. Perhaps, the friend proposed, the brothers could hold an auction and sell off furniture and other items. A livestock auctioneer named J. D. McFarland was visiting Kelowna from his home in Dawson Creek in northern British Columbia and would help arrange the sale.

The idea made sense to the brothers because, as Ken Ritchie pointed out, the jump from selling used goods to auctioneering wasn't very far. "Our father figured out that the only way to start a business when you have no money is in the secondhand business," he said.

If a guy wants to sell you something cheap, you buy it. If he wants to sell it and he wants too much for it or you haven't got the money,

Wrap 'em up, put a bow on 'em and they're gone, gone forever—he took them all!

CHAPTER ONE: THAT SECONDHAND SENSE 17

Dave, right, and John in 1941. These two would go on to run the family auction business after their older brother Ken dropped out to form his own auction house.

which is often the case, you take it on consignment. You use the same theory in the auction business. When I worked in the used goods department, we were buying and selling and pretty soon figured out that the big money was made in the buying.[15]

For their first real auction the Ritchie brothers rented Scout Hall on Bernard Avenue. They put up about $2,000 worth of stock and advertised the sale locally. Unfortunately, the sale didn't begin exactly the way the Ritchie brothers had hoped. The first item up for sale was an old pulley block.

"I had bought it for $50 and we sold it for $5," said Dave Ritchie. "I thought, 'If this is an auction, who needs it?'"[16]

The tempo soon picked up, however, when a piano that they guessed would sell for $100 actually raised $295. At the end of the day, the auction had raised $2,200. After paying the auctioneer's fee of $100 and $50 each for the rental of Scout Hall and the advertising, the Ritchie brothers were left with exactly $2,000— just the right amount to make the loan payment.

Perhaps more importantly, however, auctioneering had made a very positive impression on them. Only three weeks later, the brothers organized another auction in Scout Hall. Again they planned to sell about $2,000 in stock and hired J. D. McFarland to conduct the bidding.

On the morning of the auction, however, McFarland informed the Ritchies that his daughter had become ill in Dawson Creek and he had to leave immediately. Panic set in as the only auctioneer in town vanished north. With only an hour before the auction was to begin, the brothers searched Kelowna in vain for a replacement.

Noon came with no auctioneer, and the brothers considered canceling the event, but all the preparations were complete and they had already paid for Scout Hall. In desperation, they turned to Ken, who had practiced a little bit with McFarland. Nervously, the auctioneer started. "I remember walking that particular day from the old store, and I was hoping all the time that there was nobody going to be there," Ken Ritchie said.[17]

"Ken scrambled through the sale," John Ritchie agreed, "and I think I helped him a little bit."[18]

Shortly after the auction ended, McFarland walked into Scout Hall and announced, "Well, boys, I heard you had a very good auction."[19] In fact, he didn't have a sick daughter but had decided the brothers had the ability to auction for themselves.

The Auction Company Is Born

The Ritchie brothers had performed admirably in their first two auctions and decided to formally pursue the business opportunity. They incorporated Ritchie Bros. Auction Galleries Ltd. in 1958 to "carry on the selling of used household furniture and goods, and

All right, gentlemen, here we go... it's showtime! We've got lot number 555, triple nickel. It's a loader, knee-deep in rubber.

18   THE LEGEND OF RITCHIE BROS. AUCTIONEERS

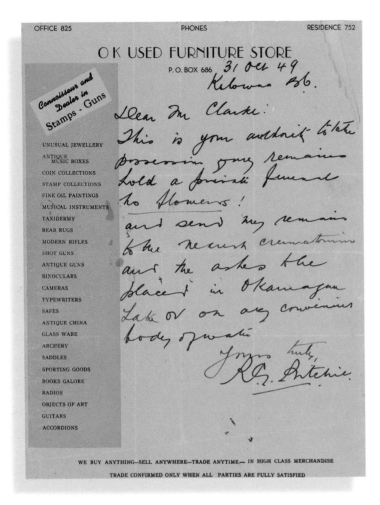

Stationary from the O.K. Used Furniture Store, with a handwritten message from Rae George Ritchie dated 1949. This secondhand store is where the Ritchie boys learned the "secondhand sense" they carried into their careers.

light industrial equipment by auction."[20] They absorbed the O.K. Used Furniture Store into the business. Dave, Ken, and John had equal shares in the company, and Ken was listed as the company president.

A year later, the brothers bought the Kelowna Furniture Company at 1618 Pandosy Street. "We paid $60,000 for the business and the building," said Dave. "We put $3,000 down, got another $10,000 by selling furniture and yet another $10,000 through auctioning off some other furniture. We were left with a mortgage at 7 percent."[21] By a quirk of fate, the building had been constructed by their grandfather, George Ritchie.

To attract customers to the new store, John hired a man to parade in front of it carrying a sandwich board that read "Prices here are too low."[22] Passersby assumed that competitors were picketing the Ritchie Bros. store because of its low prices.

Of course there were plenty of other reasons for people to come to the new building. It was a big, old building with a dumbwaiter, two levels, and a great view of the town. Before long, an informal social club formed that revolved around the brothers' various businesses and parties. Sometimes after sales, they would clear the seats and have floor hockey games, then have the floors refinished and move the furniture back into place by 6 A.M. for the opening of business. Nor was it uncommon to see visitors and Ritchies riding their bikes down the old wooden stairs, or to attend a party at which John Ritchie appeared with a shotgun and blasted stuffed sheep heads from the walls.

It was a great time for the brothers, and it was also an education for their future business lives. Years later, customers would frequently remark on the Ritchie brothers' ability to combine fun with their business and to host customers in a style that couldn't be matched. These were the years when the Ritchie brothers learned the power of a friendly relationship and absolutely erased the lines between customers and friends. A customer at the Ritchie brothers' store was automatically a friend and more often than not would find himself invited out fishing or drinking or gambling with the crew.

The auction business also began to pick up as the brothers scoured the Okanagan Valley for household deals. Soon in need of a place to hold their auctions, the brothers bought the familiar Scout Hall for $18,000. A year later, they sold it to Lipsett Motors for $20,000 and purchased the Smith Garage on Leon Avenue. They auctioned off the existing equipment,

Start me off. Who'll give me one hundred thousand dollars? Who'll bid 100, 1... 1... 100, 100, 100, you know it'll get there,

CHAPTER ONE: THAT SECONDHAND SENSE   19

then moved in their furniture business and an auction house.

"The guys put on a show," Bennett said. "I used to go to the auctions as an observer because people loved to go to the Ritchie auctions. You never knew what was going to happen or what they were going to do, and they had their patter, they had their jokes, and they interacted with the crowd very well. I guess they could be described as part businessmen, part merchandisers, and part P. T. Barnum."[23]

P. T. Barnum indeed. When the company deepfreeze was unplugged, ruining hundreds of pounds of food, including a lot of cheese, John decided to play a joke on fishermen at a local fishing derby.

We had all these labels from Japanese Airways. So I put on the radio that Ritchie Bros. Sports Shop had brought in, at considerable expense, from Japan, this Japanese commercial bait that if you go buy your tackle there that day, you can dip your plug in there. Guys would come in and say, "What is it?"

Well, I had just mixed it up that morning. It was the melted contents of our deepfreeze. I had added a quart of milk, orange crush, garlic salt, anything that made it smell bad. Then I packed it in ice and I put it in a box with an Express Japanese Airways sticker on it. One guy wanted to dip his whole tackle box in there.[24]

The auctions were by now weekly Kelowna events, with people coming as much for the atmosphere and food as for the chance to buy used goods. But they still bought, and soon the brothers became convinced that auctioneering was a big business waiting to happen. Moreover, they figured the real opportunity lay with industrial machinery, a seemingly natural

choice in a timber, construction, and mining region like Western Canada. Before long, the brothers decided to phase out used furniture and concentrate solely on machinery auctions.[25]

This decision was made easier by the greater economic forces at work during the late 1950s and early 1960s. In their home base of the Okanagan, independent sawmills and mines were closing and needed to sell their equipment. In their place, large companies like Noranda, a leader in mining and metals, and Weyerhaeuser, the lumber giant, were buying sawmills and mines to assemble land and to acquire timber rights.

Everything seemed to fall into place, and the brothers were on the path to creating a much larger business than any they had before. They began selling mill and logging equipment, borrowing $11,000 to purchase and auction off equipment from a Summerland mill. The sale brought in $24,000.[26] They soon moved on to auctions at legendary mines like Hedley, Princeton, and Copper Mountain, in addition to more sawmills at Falkland and Vernon.[27] Ken Ritchie quickly developed an affinity for sawmill sales and scoured the region looking for opportunities.

As they headed into a new decade, the brothers found themselves venturing farther and farther in quest of larger deals and bigger spreads. They were quickly learning the most important trait of any auctioneer: that secondhand sense, the instinct that enables someone to walk into a shop and quickly and thoroughly assess the value of its contents. They had to be careful, though, because their business was small, and a misplaced bid against used machinery could cost them a small fortune—and sometimes did. But they were already committed, and auctioneering quickly grew in both importance and revenue.

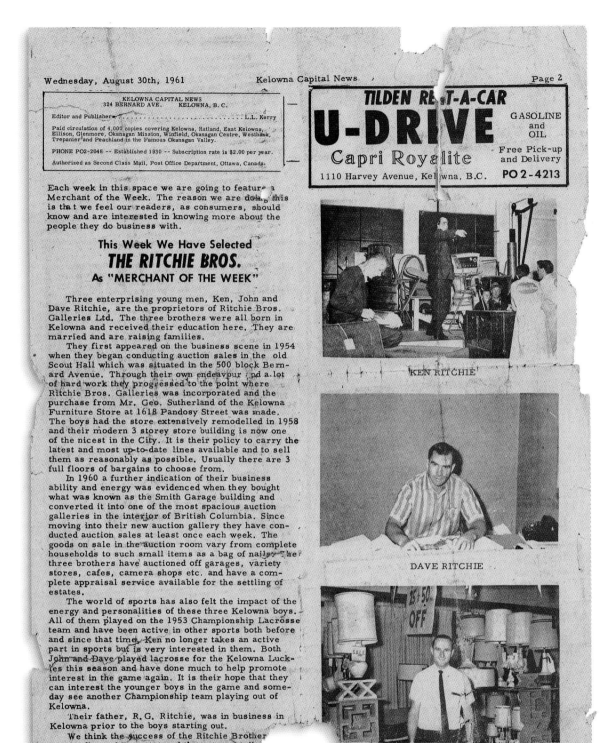

Wednesday, August 30th, 1961   Kelowna Capital News   Page 2

KELOWNA CAPITAL NEWS
324 BERNARD AVE.   KELOWNA, B.C.

Editor and Publisher .... L.L. Kerry

Paid circulation of 4,000 copies covering Kelowna, Rutland, East Kelowna, Ellison, Glenmore, Okanagan Mission, Winfield, Okanagan Centre, Westbank, Trepanier and Peachland in the Famous Okanagan Valley.

PHONE PO2-2046 -- Established 1930 -- Subscription rate is $2.00 per year.

Authorized as Second Class Mail, Post Office Department, Ottawa, Canada.

Each week in this space we are going to feature a Merchant of the Week. The reason we are doing this is that we feel our readers, as consumers, should know and are interested in knowing more about the people they do business with.

This Week We Have Selected
THE RITCHIE BROS.
As "MERCHANT OF THE WEEK"

Three enterprising young men, Ken, John and Dave Ritchie, are the proprietors of Ritchie Bros. Galleries Ltd. The three brothers were all born in Kelowna and received their education here. They are married and are raising families.

They first appeared on the business scene in 1954 when they began conducting auction sales in the old Scout Hall which was situated in the 500 block Bernard Avenue. Through their own endeavour and a lot of hard work they progressed to the point where Ritchie Bros. Galleries was incorporated and the purchase from Mr. Geo. Sutherland of the Kelowna Furniture Store at 1618 Pandosy Street was made. The boys had the store extensively remodelled in 1958 and their modern 3 storey store building is now one of the nicest in the City. It is their policy to carry the latest and most up-to-date lines available and to sell them as reasonably as possible. Usually there are 3 full floors of bargains to choose from.

In 1960 a further indication of their business ability and energy was evidenced when they bought what was known as the Smith Garage building and converted it into one of the most spacious auction galleries in the interior of British Columbia. Since moving into their new auction gallery they have conducted auction sales at least once each week. The goods on sale in the auction room vary from complete households to such small items as a bag of nails. The three brothers have auctioned off garages, variety stores, cafes, camera shops etc. and have a complete appraisal service available for the settling of estates.

The world of sports has also felt the impact of the energy and personalities of these three Kelowna boys. All of them played on the 1953 Championship Lacrosse team and have been active in other sports both before and since that time. Ken no longer takes an active part in sports but is very interested in them. Both John and Dave played lacrosse for the Kelowna Luckies this season and have done much to help promote interest in the game again. It is their hope that they can interest the younger boys in the game and someday see another Championship team playing out of Kelowna.

Their father, R.G. Ritchie, was in business in Kelowna prior to the boys starting out.

We think the success of the Ritchie Brothers outstanding achievement and they are contributing much to the economy of the City. Congratulations Ken, John and Dave.

KEN RITCHIE

DAVE RITCHIE

JOHN RITCHIE

In 1961, the hometown *Kelowna Capital News* recognized Ritchie Bros. as the Merchant of the Week.

CHAPTER TWO

FANNING OUT

1961–1964

At first in the auction business, there were a lot of games played and most auctions were because of bankruptcies. We wanted to bring credibility to the marketplace.

—Dave Ritchie, 2000

IN 1961, THE RITCHIE BROTHERS were heavily involved in the furniture business in Kelowna, although their skill in auctioneering was being increasingly recognized in the surrounding Okanagan Valley as they ventured out in search of bigger and better "spreads," or collections of property.

The *Kelowna Capital News* in its edition of August 31, 1961, recognized the trio as "The Ritchie Bros. MERCHANT OF THE WEEK." The article traced the evolution of the partnership and described both their furniture salesroom and their auction business.

The three brothers have auctioned off garages, variety stores, cafes, camera shops, etc., and have a complete appraisal service available for the settling of estates.

We think the success of the Ritchie Brothers is an outstanding achievement and they are contributing to the economy of the City.[1]

Throughout, the unique business and personal styles of the brothers continued to evolve in differing yet complementary ways. Ken was a pragmatic businessman and good auctioneer. John, also an efficient auctioneer, maintained his rowdy sense of humor and was fun,

if even slightly reckless. Dave, the youngest, had developed a vision of growing Ritchie Bros. beyond the lush Okanagan, across Canada, south into the United States, and maybe someday around the world. "This dream was great," said Ken years later, "but all we were trying to do was make an honest living."[2]

An Era Ends

Ritchie Bros.' early auction business was helped by several fundamental forces that were reshaping important industries in Western Canada. After World War II, hundreds of thousands of veterans had streamed back home to Canada hoping to buy new houses, which were made from lumber, and start families.

At the same time, the demand for fruit from the Okanagan rose, which also increased the demand for lumber because fruit was packed in wooden crates. This boom in the demand for

The Ritchie family children pictured with Ruby Beryl. Beginning clockwise from their mother are Ken, Margaret, Dave, John, and Ellen.

80, 80, give me 80, need 90, 9... 9... 9... 90 thousand, thank you! Now 1... 1... 100, bid 100, 100 thousand dollars, now up 5—

22   THE LEGEND OF RITCHIE BROS. AUCTIONEERS

lumber was answered by hundreds of newly founded, small sawmills. Called "portable sawmills," these mills could be disassembled and relocated, which enabled them to follow the supply of logs across the land after any particular region was depleted. The first portable mills were powered by steam, although in the late 1950s these were replaced by mills that ran on diesel and electricity.

However, even as they advanced technologically, the age of portable mills was drawing to a close by the late 1950s and early 1960s for a number of reasons. First and most important, larger lumber companies moved into the region and began buying the small companies, often for their timber rights more than for their equipment. As Ritchie Bros.' auction business grew beyond furniture, the company sold a lot of equipment from these suddenly defunct portable sawmills.

In 1961, as a signal that mill consolidation was there to stay, the lumber and mining giant Noranda Mines opened a subsidiary, called Northwood Mills, in the Okanagan Valley. Northwood promptly began buying smaller companies and building larger, more modern, and more efficient sawmills.

A second element working against the independent mills was the increasingly stringent regulations laid down by the British Columbia Forest Service. As the forests of British Columbia came under greater pressure from logging companies, the government stepped up its regulation of the industry. Rules were passed regarding everything from the maximum allowable amount of timber that could be cut to the amount of sawdust produced at a mill and from road-building practices to standardized wood processing. Smaller mills were often unable to comply with these requirements.

Finally, around this same time, the fruit industry switched from wooden crates to paper boxes, wiping out a major customer for smaller sawmills.

From an auctioneer's point of view, this era was ripe with opportunity—a tremendous amount of sawmill equipment was changing hands on a regular basis as the industry

The interior of the furniture store. Dave Ritchie (seen in the background) later said this was a good place to learn the business of trading and selling.

realigned itself. Ritchie Bros. began to pursue more sawmill business, ultimately developing it into a source of revenue that would last well into the 1970s.

Yet the used-equipment business was also competitive, and Ritchie Bros. strove to set itself apart. From its very first furniture sale in Scout Hall, Ritchie Bros. maintained a strict policy of unreserved auctions, meaning there were no minimum bids and absolutely no owner buybacks. The brothers were religious about this last rule, which meant that owners who contracted with Ritchie Bros. could not drive up the price of their own equipment by bidding on it.

"Everything sells to the highest bidder," said Dave Ritchie in 1999, more than 40 years after these policies had been put in place. "By contractual agreement, sellers have agreed not to bid or buy back any items. The buyers know they are guaranteed an honest auction price, at true market value."[3]

Going Places

The auction business wasn't especially hard to enter. With no permanent yards, it wasn't capital intensive—in fact, it hardly required any capital at all—and didn't need many people to run it. Auctions could be staged on leased property with a microphone. When Ritchie Bros. began pursuing equipment and sawmill auctions, it was competing against Stewart Auctions, a Calgary-based auctioneer. During this period, Dave Ritchie used to say he had "Stewartitis" because it seemed like Merv Stewart was always just leaving or just entering the offices Ritchie was visiting for business.

Although it was in the same business as Stewart, Ritchie Bros. was a very different kind of auction house. Stewart was a more traditional equipment auctioneer. The company practiced a lot more flexibility in allowing sellers to protect their prices and usually took consignments on a straight commission basis.

Ritchie Bros., on the other hand, guaranteed minimums to its consignors, meaning that if the sale didn't gross a certain amount, Ritchie Bros. would make up the difference. Offering a guaranteed minimum was an unheard-of practice because it exposed the auctioneer to risk. Ritchie Bros. was also known to purchase entire companies for the opportunity to auction off their equipment. So, although auctioneering wasn't capital intensive, Ritchie Bros. did require a steady source of financing, a fact that sometimes required a little creativity.

As a rule, Ritchie Bros. reinvested most of its earnings and maintained good relationships with its banks, but there were still times that the money simply wasn't available to finance a sale. On more than one occasion, the brothers would drive down to Vancouver and buy $30,000 or $40,000 of furniture on credit. They would take the furniture up to Kelowna, where they could sell it at auction for a small profit and, more importantly, generate cash. This money could then be used as a deposit on a much, much larger equipment auction. After that auction, they'd take the $30,000 or $40,000 back out of the sale and pay off the original furniture purchase.

This kind of thing wasn't always necessary, but it was a reflection of the nature of their business. Auctioneering wasn't like manufacturing. There were no statistical models to improve efficiency or systems that needed to be tweaked for the bottom line. Instead, there was an environment of freewheeling deal making, fueled more by personality, perseverance, and gut instinct than anything else.

The success of any auction house depended on the people running it. Sellers, who might have entrusted their live's work to Ritchie Bros., needed to feel comfortable that the company could handle the sale. Likewise, buyers had to know that Ritchie Bros. was protecting them from the unscrupulous practices typical at many other auctions.

When it came to personality, Ritchie Bros. was trebly blessed. The three brothers were a good team, even with the occasional family squabble, and all were known for their salesmanship. Yet this team wasn't seamless. Among the three brothers, there were different ideas about how to run an auction company and how big it should get. Ken, the eldest and company president, didn't want to leave the Okanagan Valley. John, who loved to hunt and fish, wanted to run the business with temporary help all summer, then collapse operations for the winter season, head south, and start the cycle back up next spring. Dave wanted to expand beyond Canadian borders, south into warmer areas, and run a full-service, year-round business.

In 1963, with this disagreement simmering, the brothers arrived at an agreement that favored growth. They would keep the O.K. Used Furniture Store in Kelowna, while each would go to a different region to establish an auction business. Dave would go to Vancouver, Ken to Calgary, and John to Edmonton.

Dave was quick to move. Early that year, he moved his family to Vancouver and rented an auction site at 4032 S.E. Marine Drive. Ken and John, however, didn't move right away.

Setting Up in Vancouver

Within months of his move, Dave Ritchie set up the company's first major auction in Vancouver. Ritchie Bros. had been contracted to sell off equipment owned by the Campbell Bennett Company. The equipment in question had been located under the Oak Street bridge in Vancouver for about six years. Ken Ritchie recalled that trees were even growing through some of the old equipment.[4]

In addition to the Campbell Bennett equipment, Ritchie Bros. sought machinery from more remote sites along the coast, including some on islands and more at the port of Prince Rupert, several hundred miles north of Vancouver. All of this was shipped by barge to the auction yard in Vancouver.

Fortunately, the relatively small sale was a success. "If that first sale would have been a bad sale," Dave Ritchie later remarked, "we'd probably be back selling furniture."[5] Instead, Dave began adjusting to his new hometown of Vancouver.

In those days of the growing lumber industry, before strict pollution controls, Vancouver was continually under a thick fog generated by beehive burners at local sawmills. It was so foggy that, as Dave recalled, "Sometimes at the end of a tow-line from a Cat, you couldn't see the guy that was hooking up at the other end."[6]

Yet Dave was committed to building a Vancouver presence. Tammy Ritchie, one of Dave Ritchie's three children, remembered moving into the Kingsway Motor Hotel as a five-year-old. "We lived there for a few months," she remembered. "We'd still go back and forth to Kelowna every weekend because all our family was there."[7]

Ken and John, meanwhile, remained in Kelowna with the furniture and luggage business and would travel for auction days. They never moved to their respective cities, a fact that never sat well with the youngest Ritchie.[8]

Ramping Up

Dave's move to Vancouver, coupled with Ritchie Bros.' growing reputation, put the company in a position to handle bigger equipment at bigger auctions. At the time, a portion of the Trans-Canada Highway project had just been completed. This tremendous undertaking was designed to lay a ribbon of highway across the breadth of the vast country, linking the Atlantic and Pacific shores of Canada.

In 1963, builders had just finished construction in the heights of the Rocky Mountains at Rogers Pass. Peter Van Vreumingen worked for the road-building company, called Premier, at the time and remembered how Ritchie pursued the sale. "Ritchie became the successful bidder on it and they had to put themselves into considerable debt, I think, to guarantee the price that they were going to realize," he said.[9]

This minimum guarantee was new in the business of auctioning heavy industrial equipment. Roland Russell, an equipment manufacturer and founder of El-Russ Equipment in Calgary, remembered Merv Stewart's reaction when he heard the Ritchie brothers had guaranteed Premier a minimum. "He came into the company I was working for saying something about how these young turkeys had come out of nowhere and here they are guaranteeing the customer a fixed figure," Russell said. "But that's how they had to break in because nobody was going to pay attention to them. After all, who were these young turks?"[10]

Ritchie Bros. won the contract and began to prepare the sale. Because of the size and volume of huge machinery involved, Ritchie Bros. planned to line up the orange machines along the new highway at a place called Radium Hot Springs in British Columbia. The auction of the heavy equipment would be conducted along this mile length of highway.

Any other Ritchie Bros. sale so far was tiny compared to this giant undertaking. The company had never tried to auction such large machinery and so much of it, and there was a strong sense of make-it-or-break-it as the auction day dawned. The Ritchie brothers had sunk almost every last penny into this sale and were counting on it. In fact, before the sale began, the company was down to only $300 in cash. Dave Ritchie took this and bought steaks and other food for a huge party after the sale—without knowing if the party was going to be a celebration or a consolation.

Unfortunately, like many days in the Canadian Rockies, that particular day dawned gray and wet. By the time the auction was to begin, a downpour opened up over the auction site, and buyers and auctioneers alike huddled in the protection of the giant equipment.

After a brief conference, the brothers decided to change their game plan. Instead of ranging along the line of equipment in a downpour, Ritchie Bros. would set up an auction area under the eve of a nearby shop building, then drive the equipment in and sell it off piece by piece. In between the sales, they would play Sousa marches to keep the crowd excited. Unbeknownst to anyone at the time, this method of auctioning heavy equipment (minus the music) would become a Ritchie

Bros. trademark, yet it was born of unfortunate necessity.

At the end of the day, despite the wet and the challenges of transporting and selling such massive equipment, it was clear the auction was an astounding success. In a single day, Ritchie Bros. had grossed $663,000—an amount that would be considered small in later years but at the time seemed almost impossible. The after-sale barbeque was likewise a huge success and, like the ramp, became a fixture at every auction. Ever since that sale at Radium Hot Springs, Ritchie Bros. has thrown a party in conjunction with almost every sale.

"That's when it became apparent to us that we could sell more in one day in the industrial auction business than we could sell in a whole year in our furniture/sporting goods store," Dave said.[11] So, in 1963, the Ritchie family sold its furniture, sporting goods, luggage, and antique business to an Alberta businessman named Hec Turvey.

The Core Team

From the very early days of their partnership, the Ritchie brothers didn't have many employees because they ran the store themselves. However, what few employees they did have were valuable additions to the team. Dick Bartel was one of the early ones. From Saskatchewan, the Bartel family had moved to the Okanagan Valley in 1947, and Dick played lacrosse with the Ritchie brothers. He began working in the Ritchie brothers' furniture store in 1957 as one of a handful of employees. Shortly after Dave moved to Vancouver, with the auction company steadily growing, Bartel decided to follow Dave, thus making him one of the auction company's original nonfamily employees. Unlike the gregarious Ritchie brothers, Bartel was a quiet and detail-minded administrator.

In Kelowna, the brothers also employed Art Lingle in the O.K. Used Furniture Store and, just after the June 7 Radium Hot Springs sale, recruited Van Vreumingen as a bookkeeper.

"It was tough, tough going in there," Ken Ritchie said.

For a while, we had only the two guys, Bartel and Lingle, working for us. The hunting season was over and one of them had to go. Art was quick on the mouth, sharp. We decided that we better stick with Lingle because Bartel was as quiet then as he is today. So we said to Bartel, "Times are tough. We're going to have to lay somebody off."

He said, "Well, I'm not doing anything. Lay me off, and I'll work for nothing."[12]

This show of loyalty induced the brothers to change their minds, and Bartel remained on staff. Shortly afterward, the successful Vancouver sale put Bartel back on the payroll.

Unfortunately, the money didn't last for long. On September 7, 1963, Ritchie Bros. followed its auction in Radium with another large-machinery event in Calgary, Alberta. The big sale was a disaster. The inexperienced brothers had purchased a spread of equipment for too much and done the worst thing an auction company could do—appraised it too high and guaranteed a minimum.

At the auction, the Ritchie brothers watched as a $40,000 loss developed. "My brothers swore they were never going back to Alberta," Dave later said.[13]

Only a week later, however, the company managed a fifth major auction, this one again located in Vancouver, and made about $70,000. It was an important and critical success as the company transitioned from smaller Kelowna-based auctions to the larger business of industrial auctions.

Van Vreumingen described some of the company's early practices:

I used to do the books. For me, with the weekly sales still in Kelowna, it was almost like working for a second-hand dealer. I didn't feel that I belonged there, and I quit two or three times. Every time, the brothers talked me into staying. But they all had different personalities,

and as their accountant, I had to listen to three bosses. And they would always rob me of my petty cash. I would come in the office in the morning and the petty cash would be sitting empty with an IOU from one of them.

Then they might have a little fight amongst themselves and one would quit and ask me to do his final paycheck and give me his company credit card. I got to the point where I didn't even listen to them. I would just put those credit cards in my drawer because I would know that a few days later, the others would ask him to come back.[14]

The Ritchie Auction

Clearly, the future of the company did not lie with the smaller sales in Kelowna. Ken and John had continued to hold regular auctions every Thursday night, selling furniture, household goods, boats, and all kinds of miscellaneous stuff. It wasn't a lot of money, but it gave the company a decent cash flow.

In Vancouver, however, Dave Ritchie was pursuing much more lucrative spreads in the heavy equipment business. Less than a year after moving to Vancouver, he rented property at 443 Vanguard Road in Richmond. The site contained a mechanical shop, an office, and an auction site, all located only minutes across the Oak Street bridge from Vancouver.

Ritchie Bros. also continued honing the auction style that would distinguish it among its competitors. While the most important element of the business was the unreserved auction policies, the company also paid close attention to the events themselves. A Ritchie Bros. sale was a careful blend of good business opportunities, friendly personnel, and a circus atmosphere as buyers were invited to both participate in and simply enjoy the high-stakes, fast-moving drama of a large auction.

Beth Farrell, an early Ritchie Bros. employee who once acted as a contortionist in vaudeville theater, described a good auction as a stage production: "You have your opening

Bidder number 1472. The good bidders are certainly here today.

CHAPTER TWO: FANNING OUT   27

act, your feature, and your closing. I know whether we've done a good show or not."[15]

And, true to form, the show didn't end when the last lot was sold. After their auctions, the brothers continued to gather everybody for a big steak cookout or barbeque, complete with cold beer and live music. As the years went on, this traditional party was held before the auctions so customers who came into town could attend without worrying about their postauction travel plans. Like the sales themselves, these parties were an important part of the overall event because they provided an opportunity to make contacts and simply have some fun.

"We would sometimes sit with 30 or more people in the early days," Van Vreumingen said. "Even out there in the bush, like with Radium Hot Springs, they would just set up and have steaks and barbeque."[16]

Beginning with that sale at Radium Hot Springs, Ritchie Bros. adopted the ramp-and-stage approach for selling all of its mobile equipment. The staging area was designed so the ramp was located in the front of a viewing stadium, where buyers sat waiting for the parade of Big Iron to come steaming onto the stage. Each piece of equipment was numbered and, once it came to rest, an auctioneer, often Ken or John Ritchie, began asking for bids.

"John was the quintessential heavy equipment seller," recalled Vic Walls, a customer who began attending Ritchie auctions in the 1960s. "He could knock down heavy equipment in a manner that I've never seen anybody match. And he did things that were absolutely dramatic to get the crowd's attention."[17]

As the prices were called, the crowd was closely watched by roving bid catchers, who signaled the auctioneer when a bid was made. During bidding, Ritchie Bros. was also known for conducting a fast sale. Some other auctioneers, knowing they weren't making their spreads, would harangue the crowd for more bids and draw out bidding endlessly until the price was raised. At a Ritchie sale, the bids were called, and if no more were forthcoming

The company went to great lengths to take care of its bidders, even handing out complimentary umbrellas on rainy days.

in about a minute or so, the equipment was sold to the highest bidder.

"In those early days, John did a lot of the bid calling," remembered Western Canadian equipment dealer Matt Campbell, who began attending Ritchie auctions in the early 1970s. "When he'd see the crowd getting sleepy, he'd sell something real quick and everybody would wake right up, thinking, 'I missed that! I missed that!' It really began to forge the modern method of auctioneering."[18]

OK, now listen to me, gentlemen, we've got five tractors on the ramp, we're selling choice.

Lots 672, 673, 674, 675 and 676. Who'll give me fifty thousand, 50, 50 do it quickly...

Erecting colorful tents to protect people from the weather, the brothers believed in creating a fun atmosphere that encouraged camaraderie.

After all the mobile equipment was sold, the auctioneer, stationed in a specially built booth on the back of a pickup truck, led prospective bidders along the rows of large cranes or other pieces of immobile equipment.

Throughout all this action, the air was laced with the mingled smells of diesel and frying hamburgers and onions. Like the parties, Ritchie Bros. auctions established themselves as a gathering place for Canada's dealers and aficionados of heavy machinery, who judged prices, bought, sold, and socialized at the carefully orchestrated events.

"Going to them auctions is kind of like going to a good funeral," said Bill Bremmeyer, a long-time friend of the Ritchie brothers. "You see all them people you haven't seen in a long time."[19]

The Bones of the Deal

Another critical ingredient in the success of an auction—and the auction company that appraised it—was the equipment itself. Ritchie was always looking for good opportunities, and for many of the first equipment sales, a retired Kelowna contractor named Jack Serwa helped appraise the spreads. "Serwa was clever enough to know about equipment dealing and was a real big help," said Ken Ritchie in 2000. "He is still sorely missed around the company."[20]

By teaching the boys how to appraise equipment, Serwa was arming them for success in the future. Appraisal was not only critical to Ritchie Bros.' profit because of the guaranteed minimums; it was also of critical importance to the consignors. John Reid, logging manager of Cattermole Contractors in British Columbia in 1965, started placing equipment in Ritchie auctions in 1965 and, almost 35 years later, sold out his own company in a Ritchie auction. "Ritchie will come in and look at a spread and they'll come up with a number," Reid said. "They're probably pretty close."[21]

Assuming the appraisal was acceptable to the consignor, Ritchie Bros. offered a number of different contract options for the actual sale.

The first option, and least complicated, was the straight commission deal. In this kind of auction, Ritchie charged a straight commission of between 8 and 20 percent on the sale value of the items it auctioned off. The majority of Ritchie's business came from straight commission auctions, and it was the most common form of contract in the auction business.

Consignors could also opt for the guaranteed minimum. At the time, Ritchie Bros. was perhaps the only equipment auctioneer in North America to offer this choice. Consequently, because it carried higher risk, Ritchie Bros. charged a higher commission. On sale day, if the actual gross sales exceeded the guaranteed minimum, the additional money was split on a negotiated basis.

Finally, the last option was for Ritchie Bros. to purchase the equipment outright. While this definitely carried the highest risk, it also resulted in the highest-profit sales.

Once the contract was signed, Ritchie began advertising the auction to prospective buyers and advising the consignor on how to present his equipment for the maximum possible purchase price. Machinery to be auctioned was often sandblasted and repainted before the sale day.

In 1963, the year of the Radium sale, the Ritchies conducted a total of eight auctions ranging from Little Fort in northern British Columbia to Calgary, Vancouver, and even their hometown of Kelowna. By the end of its first year in Vancouver, the auction company boasted gross sales of more than $1 million, much of that figure due to the Radium Hot Springs sale.

One Brother Short

With sales like this, it might have seemed that Dave Ritchie's sales skill was beyond question. But such was not the case. In March 1964, after a fight with his brothers over a deal in northern Canada, Dave failed a salesmanship test. The really interesting part, however, was why Dave Ritchie found himself taking a test of his sales abilities in the first place: He had just been fired by his brothers.

"I had bought a deal up north," he remembered of the situation.

It was a big package for Bedford Construction. When I moved to Vancouver, I joined the Canadian Creditman's Trust Association, which was a credit-granting agency and told me who was in trouble. If some contractor or construction outfit or logger was in trouble, he was a potential customer. I happened to be sitting there when this name Bedford Construction came up, so I got to meet a fellow by the name of Bernie Lovis, who was the general manager.

He wouldn't hardly give me the time of day, but I figured out the parent company was a dredge and dock company out of Toronto. So I got ahold of a fellow back in Toronto and told him I was interested in buying the spread they had up on the Stewart Cassiar Highway, way up in north British Columbia. It was a project that had basically just gone broke. I took Jack Serwa up there with me to look at it. The equipment was buried in snow, and we reviewed it all. I came back down and made a deal with the parent corporation.[22]

To Dave, it seemed like a sound deal. To Ken and John, who had been listening to a couple old timers from the north who didn't think it was such a great deal, it seemed like a disaster. They banded together and fired their younger brother. In need of a job, Dave went to a finance company called IAC and applied for a job.

"They filled out this big, bloody form, and they gave me this sales aptitude test," said Dave Ritchie. "I guess I was still full of myself because I thought I was the best salesman in the world. I thought I had done everything right on the whole test. But I went back on Thursday, and they said, 'This thing proves you're not suitable for sales.' I had already been making a living at it all my life. I was really in a state of shock."[23]

He had, after all, been selling every auction three times: once to his customers, once to his brothers, and once to the bank. Yet now he was out of a career. By this time, however, John and Ken had gone up north to look at the spread for themselves and decided it wasn't such a bad deal after all. They asked Dave to return to the company, but he was still so angry that he came back only to help sell the spread (which he had bought for $175,000) for $385,000. That night, with Dave back at the company, they backed up the sound truck into an old hall for music and threw a wild party. And ever since, Dave Ritchie has discouraged the use of personality and aptitude tests at the company.

In Vancouver, Ritchie Bros. opened a small business office in the commercial heart of the city at 558 Howe Street. Bartel and Dave Ritchie, plus a secretary, worked there in an unpretentious office and began to make the contacts that would serve them later. Among these was a financial officer named John Wild, who often provided financing and financial services to the buyers at Ritchie Bros.' auctions. Wild, who would ultimately join Ritchie Bros. in the early 1980s, remembered lunching with Bartel and Dave and gambling with the two to see who would pay the lunch bill.[24]

"I never won, and I could never quite figure it out," Wild said. "Later on, I did figure it out. They didn't have any money in those days and I was on expenses, so I could afford to buy the lunches."[25]

The Ritchie Bros. auction sale brochure, advertising items for sale, became a calling card for the company.

CHAPTER THREE

EXPANSION IN THE AIR

1965–1973

You need to love the business. It doesn't mean it's not work. I work hard, but to me, it's a holiday camp.

—Dave Ritchie, 2000

THROUGHOUT THE EARLY 1960s, the lumber industry in British Columbia continued to grow and consolidate as the demand for lumber increased. And, at the time, it seemed that British Columbia had an inexhaustible supply of high-quality lumber. Forests covered more than two-thirds of the province's almost 375,000 square miles. Together with mining, forestry employed 25 percent of the workforce in British Columbia between the years 1964 and 1979.

The flux in these two industries helped Ritchie Bros., which was never far behind. "Any time a mine closed down or anything like that or a mill closed, it affected the whole community," said Dave Ritchie. "The people were leaving, and you could buy anything they had to sell. My brother and I would go door to door and buy everything. We had a big old five-ton truck that we'd load up and drive back to Kelowna."[1]

These no-minimum, unreserved auctions soon began to attract a kind of customer-consignor that might have otherwise shunned auctions, which at the time had a reputation for being rigged for the owners and the auction company.

Roland Russell experienced firsthand the company's commitment to an honest auction. A ticklish situation developed during a sale in Alberta, when Ritchie Bros. had bought out a contractor named Al Sprecker. Russell, who was friends with Sprecker, bought a piece of equipment that had belonged to Sprecker and, before he had even wired Ritchie Bros. the money, received a phone call from the contractor.

Al called me on a Sunday and said, "Roland, you can't believe what just happened to me. I've been working on a deal with a big oil company for the past five years and they just called and said it's mine. You bought one of the crushing plants, so what kind of deal could I make with you to get it back?"

I told him that I hadn't paid and I was going to wire Ritchie the money on Monday. It still wasn't on our books. So I told him he could have it back and he owed me a good lunch the next time I saw him.

Ritchie Bros. specialized in heavy equipment, like the kind used in sawmills and mines, but would sell anything that needed selling, including trucks, campers, and even whole buildings.

for choice, 125, 25, 25... last chance... 125... SOLD to your man, Eddie, for one hundred and twenty thousand dollars.

34   THE LEGEND OF RITCHIE BROS. AUCTIONEERS

Then, of course, I get this phone call from Dave Ritchie. He says, "Roland, what the hell kind of games are you playing?" His concern was that I bought it back for Sprecker. So I told him the story and he believed it, but he said he had to check it out because it would be a conflict of their company culture.[2]

It would be hard to overstate how important this reputation was to Ritchie Bros.' growing business. "The reputation of auctions, until Ritchie came along, was not that great," said Matt Campbell of Hammer Equipment, a second-generation equipment dealer.

It was a pretty dirty business. Frequently you were bidding against the vendor. Unreserved auctions just weren't being done, even though some guys would advertise that it was unreserved. There were even occasions in the history of auctions where the auction company would auction off a contractor's lifetime earnings and disappear with the money. But the Ritchie brothers established their reputation pretty quick. People knew they were actually doing what they said they were going to do.[3]

This reputation is due directly to the Ritchie brothers themselves. Many people recall seeing Dave Ritchie forcibly respond to buyers who were bidding on their own equipment. Likewise, said Terry Simpson of Pacific Forklift, "I've seen Dave Ritchie stop the sale and go up to a person and say, 'Do you own this piece of equipment?' If they admitted they did or Ritchie knew that he did, the company announced that the seller was bidding on his own machine, and the sale continued with one less bidder in the crowd."[4]

Beyond British Columbia

Although Ritchie Bros. was headquartered in British Columbia, Dave Ritchie hoped to move the company across Canada. This ambition was particularly well suited to the business of Big Iron. Industrial machinery, like airplanes, tended to have a long life. Owners of the expensive machines often maintained them scrupulously. Moreover, large earth moving equipment and cranes were often needed during a particularly large project, but there was no permanent need for them in the region. In fact, as transoceanic shipping became more affordable and easier, a single piece of equipment might travel the world several times over, moving from job to job and contractor to contractor.

Moreover, Dave Ritchie figured that a geographic strategy had its own built-in protection for Ritchie Bros., which could move equipment from depressed regions to hungry markets. In addition, buyers would come from far-flung regions to buy locally and transport their purchases to where the next construction contract lay, whether it involved pipelines or highways or dams.

Yet building a global auction business was a departure from the normal business model. At the time, there were no worldwide industrial-equipment auction houses. The business was dominated by a few regional companies and even fewer national companies. Yet Ritchie Bros. followed a business model different from other auctioneers—something that was apparent from the earliest days.

Frank W. Forst, who described himself as "the world's greatest salesman," attended his first Ritchie Bros. auction in the early 1960s. He would attend at least one Ritchie Bros. auction every year for the next three decades in the course of buying and selling industrial equipment all around the world.

"The first sale, I was buying scrapers for highway construction in Venezuela," Forst remembered.

From day one, they ran the most organized auction. They started on time and moved along in an organized way. The company is very honest and innovative. They have altered the entire machinery industry, and they are religious about no buybacks. At one time auctions were thought of as wholesale. They have made it into a retail business.[5]

DIAMOND DAVE

IN 1969, WHILE LOOKING FOR A GOOD spread for auction, Dave Ritchie ran into an interesting deal. A diamond drilling company called Deeg Drilling in the interior of British Columbia was headed for bankruptcy.

Ritchie bought the equipment, originally intending to put it up for auction—until he looked at the operation. It turned out that Deeg had gone bankrupt for a pretty simple reason. The company had run water lines all over the side of a mountain. These lines were supposed to feed the drills, but they were prone to crimping. When this happened, the flow of water would stop and the drill would shut down, costing valuable production.

So John and Dave Ritchie put their heads together and decided to go into mineral drilling. They figured they would dig reservoirs next to each site and eliminate the need for water hoses, thus creating an efficient and steady drilling operation. It worked. They soon incorporated the new company as Tonto Drilling (as in "Heigh ho, Silver," because they were looking for valuable minerals) and went to work.

Dave Ritchie spent about a year working this company to get it running, then sold it to Chuck Croft, a future director of Ritchie Bros. Tonto Drilling later became a successful, worldwide exploration company.

In 1964, in only its second year of business, Ritchie Bros. was already expanding beyond British Columbia. That summer, the company staged a sale in Edmonton, Alberta. Only three months later, the company headed north and put together a sale in Watson Lake in the Yukon. By the end of the year, Ritchie Bros. had conducted 10 auctions with revenue of $1.4 million.

Beginning its third year, however, the three-way partnership splintered somewhat. Ken Ritchie, company president and the eldest, didn't want to travel so much and had essentially never left Kelowna. He wanted to stay in the Okanagan Valley, where his family lived and where he had grown up. In late 1965, he sold his shares to his brothers. As he left, the company's name was changed from Ritchie Bros. Auction Galleries Ltd. to Ritchie Bros. Auctioneers Ltd. Ken couldn't stay away from auctioneering, however. Within 18 months, he had founded another company called Ken Ritchie Auctions, located in the Okanagan Valley. It was a direct competitor to the larger Ritchie Bros. Auctioneers Ltd.

In the time leading up to Ken's departure, Ritchie Bros. prospered. Sales in 1965 almost doubled, reaching $2.4 million, and the company held its first auction in Saskatchewan with an event at Kindersley. By the end of the year, Ritchie Bros. was active in British Columbia, Alberta, Saskatchewan, and the Yukon Territory.

In the Yukon, Ritchie Bros. held a second sale that summer when Leo Proctor, a well-known contractor with mining interests, contracted to liquidate his entire construction fleet. It included vehicles, crawler tractors, earthmovers, loaders, and sawmill equipment, and buyers from Alaska to Toronto flew in to attend the auction.

Like every Ritchie Bros. sale, this auction was held at a leased site and followed a by-now-familiar pattern. With a contract in hand, the brothers flew to the location, found a good yard, rented it, and adapted it for a major auction. Invariably, this included building the trademark Ritchie Bros. ramp for the heavy machinery to rumble across during auction. Next, the brothers scouted out local financial

36   THE LEGEND OF RITCHIE BROS. AUCTIONEERS

companies, transportation, and temporary help to handle the actual sale.

With the site prepared and the initial spread of equipment in line, Ritchie Bros. began promoting the sale, both to potential buyers and to other contractors who might have equipment to sell. The marketing always included a brochure that listed what was available and innumerable phone calls and visits to equipment yards. The goal was to get the greatest amount of good equipment possible, bring in buyers from anywhere, and attract as much attention as possible.

"Every major sale we had in a new area, we'd go through the phone book and collect names and addresses of contractors and buy mailing lists to make sure that we'd get that industry," said Dick Bartel. "We'd do a special mailing, and the direct mail was by far the best. We could do a lot of newspaper advertising, but by sending out that flyer for every sale that we had, every customer would get it in the mailbox."[6]

The company was willing to try anything to advertise its sales. Before one trucking sale, the Canadian postal service went on strike right before the brochures were mailed out. The brothers simply put together a telex and transmitted it to every trucking company they could find, making the companies feel special and getting the word out.

For another sale, Dave and John decided to fly a hot-air balloon over the yard so customers could easily find the site. "We thought we'd get a great big balloon and hang a Ritchie Bros. flag on it," said Dave Ritchie.

A piece of "yellow iron," as used equipment is known in the heavy equipment trade. This piece of machinery came from M.E.L. Construction, an early major consignor at Ritchie Bros.' auctions.

good news for you. I have two left and your man was runner-up, he was with us all the way, does he want one? The money

CHAPTER THREE: EXPANSION IN THE AIR 37

THE SINGING AUCTIONEER

THE MOST VISIBLE PART OF ANY auction company is the auctioneer himself. These colorful characters are the voice behind the sales, chanting a cadence over the crowd to solicit bids and promote machinery. In the early days, Ken and John Ritchie did most of the auctioneering themselves, but before long the company began to hire contract auctioneers. Perhaps the most famous of these was Wayne Clark, nicknamed "Leroy" after the famous country-and-western singer.

"A certain fever often comes over the people during the auction," said Clark. "It's when the bidding starts to get hot that the auctioneer really feels in his element."[1]

Clark, an auctioneer who yodeled, cajoled, sang, and promoted, was comfortable in his element, remarkable considering that he had become an auctioneer quite by accident. He was attending a cattle auction in the 1950s when he discovered the auctioneer had never shown up. The organizers of the auction, knowing he was an entertainer, asked him to conduct the auction. "The fellows plied me with rum and coke, and pretty soon I was auctioning off cattle," he remembered.[2]

Not long afterward, Clark discovered he had a natural aptitude for auctioneering. He attended the Reisch School of Auctioneering in Mason City, Iowa, and in 1966 began to work with Ritchie Bros.

"He was really good at it," said Dick Bartel. "He had the humor to go with it, and he could convince the crowd that they were getting fair deals and that if there was something there that's going to be sold cheaply, they would have a chance to buy it."[3]

is one hundred and twenty thousand, sir. SOLD! Bidder number 1689. He takes which one? He takes the front one...

38   THE LEGEND OF RITCHIE BROS. AUCTIONEERS

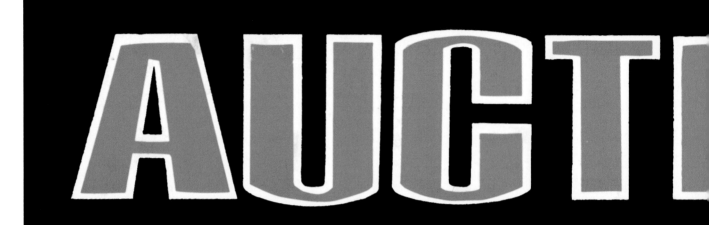

UNRESERVED SALE • THE HIGH

2 LARGE SPREADS IN ONE GI

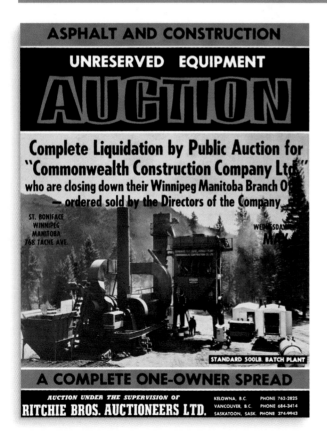

So we hired this professional air balloon company, and I remember talking to John Ivester, the guy who runs The Last Bid magazine, and I see this crew. They look very professional. They come out. They had a tarp, put it down, and brought the balloon out. They blew it up, and it gets to be a nice big balloon. I went inside for something, and when I came back out I see this balloon going away. I think, 'We don't want it way up there; no one will ever see it.' So I go to the truck to tell them to bring it down, but they're all standing there saying, "Well, I thought you had it." "No, you had it."

We had to call the airport and tell them the balloon was coming by.[7]

Left and above: Ritchie Bros.' unreserved auctions quickly gained a reputation as honest and legitimate ways to buy and sell used equipment. With this reputation forming, the company pursued ever larger spreads of equipment. In 1968, Dave Ritchie put together a big sale for Commonwealth Construction Company in Manitoba (left).

lot 673. OK, I have one left. The price is 120. Who wants it at 120? Take it now or I'll open it up. First hand... SOLD! Bidder number?

CHAPTER THREE: EXPANSION IN THE AIR   39

Typically, though, every year the company would score one or two big "wins" that translated into more growth. In 1967, Dave Ritchie put together a big win in Manitoba for the old Carter Construction Company. The goods involved equipment, buildings, and real estate. Dave bought the deal near Christmas, when the snowpack was high enough to hide the spring flood marks six feet high on the buildings.

"I felt pretty good about it, but then I started finding out about the flooding," Dave said. "It didn't bother us. If it had, if I had really known, I probably would never have been so gutsy."[8]

The sale was held in May and grossed about $400,000.

Edmonton also quickly emerged as an important auction market and, on April 26, 1968, was the site of the first Ritchie Bros.' auction that grossed more than $1 million in a single sale. More than 1,000 people attended this event to bid on equipment from several large contractors.

Even with the bigger sales, it didn't take many people to run a multimillion-dollar auction house. The staff was still limited to about a dozen full-time employees—including Ken Ritchie, whom the brothers were happy to welcome back in 1968.

"After starting my own business, I found Ritchie Bros. to be very tough competition and got back to work with them as fast as I damn well could," Ken Ritchie said.[9] His son, Mike Ritchie, would eventually join the company and become a partner.

"Some of my first memories are of attending the auctions with my father," Mike said.

One particular trip was to Williams Lake, British Columbia, approximately 200 miles from home in Kelowna. Father, Dick Bartel, and I were headed down a particularly steep hill on the highway 97C where it meets the Trans-Canada just west of Kamloops. It was the day before a sale, and in the back of the pickup we had the auctioneer's podium and a desk for the accountant, Mr. Peter Van Vreumingen. As we went down the hill picking up speed, the desk flew out and bounced into the ditch, smashing into 1,000 pieces. Peter was not very happy when he saw his desk.[10]

South to the United States

By the end of the 1960s, Ritchie Bros. Auctioneers had grown far beyond what the sporting goods store and furniture company could ever have become. Yet it was still a regional company, basically limited to Western Canada, with a couple sales every year in Eastern Canada. More importantly, at least to Dave Ritchie, the company had no presence in the United States.

"Many customers from the U.S. were attending our Canadian sales, so it was a natural extension of our company to grow into those markets," Dave Ritchie remarked. "A lot of the money being spent at Ritchie Bros. auctions was American."[11]

In 1969, the company was ready for a first move across the border. That year, Ritchie Bros.

Bidder number, please... number 915, thank you. Well done. They're going fast today!

40   THE LEGEND OF RITCHIE BROS. AUCTIONEERS

Above and left: As Ritchie Bros. grew, its geographic scope and expertise in equipment grew also. By the late 1960s, the company was active throughout Western Canada, selling equipment used for all sorts of purposes. These rollers were sold in 1964 for the Nadon Paving Company in Edmonton. Incidentally, the Nadon sale was also one of the first at which Ritchie Bros. auctioned off real estate.

Opposite: This newspaper advertisement was placed in a local paper to attract attention to an auction sale at Prince George. Even from the earliest days, Ritchie Bros. undertook extensive advertising campaigns to attract buyers to its sales.

incorporated in Washington state to carry on the sale of used equipment[12]—and quickly found out that the business regulations in the United States were different from those in Canada. In the United States, the laws governing auctions were made on a state-by-state basis, and in some states, auctions could be conducted only by U.S. citizens or a state resident.

To remedy this, Dave recruited Dick Williams, a U.S. resident, and gave him 25 percent of the United States company. The remainder was split among Dave, John, and Dick Bartel. As it turned out, Williams was a great guy and a "hell of a joke teller," but not too loyal.[13] He had pretty good knowledge of the equipment business and was a decent auctioneer, and as "soon as the business got going pretty good, Dick Williams would quit and start up his own company." Yet Williams didn't have success on his own, and he always came back to Ritchie Bros. for a job. Ultimately, Williams quit and was rehired three times, a record for any senior Ritchie Bros. employee except the brothers.

When Ritchie Bros. moved into the United States, the company was entering a market already claimed by several other companies. Most prominent among these were Forke Brothers, based in Nebraska, and Miller and Miller, based in Texas. Both companies had excellent reputations and established connections in the United States and were not inclined to let an outsider pry open their market. Ritchie Bros., which was the only auction company in the United States willing to offer a guaranteed minimum, accelerated the already fierce competition for the country's rich auction grounds.

"The first year in the United States wasn't bad," Dave Ritchie later told *Truck/Logger* magazine. "But the second year we lost a lot of money. [My brothers] were convinced that we would never make money in the United States."[14]

The brothers' disagreement would have deep implications for the immediate future of Ritchie Bros. Auctioneers because the company was still growing strongly with Canadian sales and Ken and John didn't want to pull away from this lucrative business. In 1971, for example, Ritchie Bros. put together an important and successful sale for Burntwood Construction of Manitoba. The sale was one of the first tax-sheltered deals put together by Ritchie Bros. and benefited both Ritchie and Ron Coleman, the

---

Ritchie Bros. INDUSTRIAL AUCTIONEERS

Offer by Public Auction at Unreserved Sale

CONSTRUCTION EQUIPMENT

Name of owner: BEN GINTER CONSTRUCTION CO. LTD.

PLACE: Goglin Rd. Prince George, B.C.	DATE: August 8 10:00 a.m.

10 CRAWLER TRACTORS — 3 Cats D9G, Model 66A, S/N 2008, 2000 and 306, c/w Hyd. U-Dozers, Rippers, Draw Bars, Etc. 5 Caterpillars D8, 46As, S/Ns 10245, 8298, 7340, 7279, and 7280 c/w Hyd. U-Dozers and Rippers. 1 Caterpillar D7E, 48A, S/N 5685 c/w Hyd. Dozer, Hyster Winch. 2 Euclid Tractors, Model 8240 and C6 c/w Hyd. Dozers and Winches.

6 MOTOR GRADERS — 2 Caterpillar Model 14Ds, 4 Adams Model 666's.

7 FRONT END LOADERS — 1967 Scoopmobile Model 1200 complete with 10 yd. bucket. 4 Hough Models H120C, H-120C, H120B, and H100. 1 Caterpillar 966B. 1 Caterpillar 977 Crawler Model 53A.

5 MOTOR SCRAPERS — 5 Caterpillar 631B Motor Scrapers, 13G Tractors and 11G Scrapers. 3 Caterpillar Model 80 Pull Scrapers (Series 2D).

5 END DUMPS — 3 Euclid Model 91F End Dumps. 2 — 1962 Euclid rear dumps, S/N 30751 & 30753 powered by G.M.C. 6110 engines, 18:00 x 25 tires, 18 cu. yd. box.

DRAGLINES & CRANES — Michigan Model T20 15-Ton Truck Crane. 1964 Northwest Model 250 Crawler Crane c/w Boom and Backhoe. 1964 P & H Model 525 Crawler Crane. **30 TRUCKS** — Including late model pick-ups, service trucks, company cars, 4x4s, 1-Tons, tandems, truck tractors.

AIR EQUIPMENT — Gardener-Denver 900 CFM Compressor-mounted on G.M.C. Tandem Truck. Gardner-Denver Air Trac 300 Series complete with 123 Hammer. LeRoi Tractair 105 CFM Compressor.

ASPHALT EQUIPMENT—Barber-Greene 840B Asphalt Plant complete with Drier Unit, Graduation Unit, and Pug Mill Unit, Barber-Greene 879B Paver, Childers Hot Oil Heater, Etnyre Distributor, etc.

MISCELLANEOUS EQUIPMENT — Includes Case Tractor, Snowmobile, Noble 6 yd. Weigh Batcher, Cement Equipment, Hydraulic Diggers, 1967 Tel-e-ect Hydraulic Auger and Miscellaneous Camp Equipment, Sheepsfoot Packers.

thousand and go, 200, 200, two hundred thousand, 200, 200, OK, we'll do this the hard way, one hundred thousand, 100, 100, now

42   THE LEGEND OF RITCHIE BROS. AUCTIONEERS

UNRESERVED EQUIPMENT AUCTION

TUESDAY MAY 4th 10 A.M. RED DEER, ALBERTA

1970 HEWITT ROBINS CONE CRUSHER

GOOD - CLEAN LATE MODEL EQUIPMENT!

1970 HOUGH MODEL 120-C LOADER

**ON BEHALF OF
BODEN BROS. CONSTRUCTION LTD.
KELLYS CONSTRUCTION LTD.
BORDEN TRANSPORT LTD.
BOTT CONSTRUCTION LTD.**

FEATURE ITEMS

1970 HEWITT ROBINS CONE CRUSHER
1970 HOUGH 120 C LOADER
1969 CAT 977 K LOADER
2 - 1969 CAT D8 46A's
1970 500 KW POWER TRAILER
2 - 1969 WHITE FREIGHT LINERS
LATE MODEL COMPACTION ITEMS
ROLLERS - VIBRATORY PACKERS
1969 CAT D6C - 10K MODEL
LATE MODEL LOW BEDS - HI BOYS
ROLLS - JAW - CRUSHERS
5 - 1970 PORTABLE CONVEYORS
1970 PICKUPS - SERVICE TRUCKS

TUES - MAY 4th 10 A.M.

NO RESERVES — NO LIMITS — 4 COMPLETE SPREADS!

RITCHIE BROS. AUCTIONEERS LTD.

KELOWNA, B.C.
246 Lawrence Ave.
Telephone (604) 762-2825

VANCOUVER, B.C.
558 Howe Street
Telephone (604) 682-1366

CALGARY, ALBERTA
4320 Dalhousie Drive N.W.
Telephone (403) 288-8791

EDMONTON, ALBERTA
3824 - 112th Street
Telephone (403) 435-9111

Opposite: Red Deer, Alberta, became an important auction ground in the late 1960s and early 1970s. Home to M.E.L. Construction, in addition to other contractors, the region produced some high-grossing sales.

company's owner. Ritchie Bros. ended up buying the whole company, not just the equipment.

"We could structure a deal in so many ways," said Dave Ritchie. "We were imaginative to figure things out, and that was a big separation between us and everybody else."[15]

A year later, with the Vancouver operation growing so quickly under Dave Ritchie, the company headquarters were moved from Kelowna, where John Ritchie still kept his office, to Vancouver. Before the move, Dave Ritchie approached Peter Van Vreumingen, who had been the bookkeeper for almost a decade, and asked him to move also. But Van Vreumingen was not interested.

"At that time, I was in my fifties, and I didn't really want to move to the coast with all the rain and all you see is construction yards and airplanes and airports," Van Vreumingen said. "Also, I had been away from home at least 12 days every month. In the meantime, Dave said, 'We'll bend over backwards to keep you.' But I told my wife I would find something else and quit."[16]

When he quit, Ritchie Bros. was a much larger company than the one he had joined. Besides the new office in Portland, Oregon, Ritchie Bros. had a presence in Calgary, an office in Saskatoon run by Bert Sutton, and another in Edmonton run by Bill Gronberg, who had joined in the late 1960s.

"I think Bill Gronberg deserves a lot of the credit for the way the Ritchies present their auc-

tion sales, where everything is lined up neat as a pin," remarked Matt Campbell, an equipment dealer and family friend. "He's a perfectionist, and I remember he was really front and center in Edmonton for a long time. When he ran an auction, everything was swept clean and tidy and neat. You could run a string down a line of dozers and they would be just absolutely perfect."[17]

When Van Vreumingen announced he was leaving the company, Ritchie Bros. needed a new bookkeeper and turned to Russ Cmolik, a young accountant with the company's auditors who was working toward his articles. The company had been contracting with Cmolik since 1968 to help Van Vreumingen. Cmolik remembered the offer: "They came to my firm, and the firm said to me, 'What do you think?' I said, 'Sure, it sounds good.' I then started going to auctions and to their office and filling in, doing title searching and going out on some deals with David."[18]

Like all the Ritchie Bros. employees, Cmolik had grown up in Kelowna and knew the Ritchie brothers. His parents were friends with Ken Ritchie and regular customers at both the company's auctions and its sporting goods store.

"One of my earliest recollections of Ritchie is my dad bought me a hockey stick as a gift," Cmolik said. "It was one of my very first real store-bought hockey sticks. I was probably ten or eleven, and the first shot I made with the stick, it broke. I was devastated, but I scored a goal because the blade of the stick went one way and the puck went the other and the goalie stopped the blade instead of the puck. Afterward, my dad and I trotted down to the Ritchies, and they just plucked another stick out. Didn't even ask a question."[19]

Cmolik earned his articles in 1972 and joined Ritchie Bros. on March 1, 1973.

The Surrey auction yard. This was Ritchie Bros.' first permanent yard. Dave Ritchie is standing on the raised platform in the center, and the Pattullo Bridge is in the background.

CHAPTER FOUR: CHANGING OF THE GUARD   47

by the Tax Department."[4] So he sold his 50 percent of the shares to Dave and, to protect himself from a tax liability, converted some of his assets into gold and moved his family to South Africa. Later, he recalled, "I was looking for a country. I took my family and left Canada because I was red flagged."[5] For his legacy, he left scores of people who would never forget his style and force of personality. He also left some gold on the Ritchie Bros. Auctioneers balance sheet.[6] (Interestingly, his decision to convert company assets into gold was similar to his father's preference of having his pension checks paid in silver dollars.)

For Dave Ritchie, consolidating ownership of the company translated into freedom to continue expansion into the United States and the challenges that entailed, including immigration issues.

"We were very, very careful," said Cmolik of an early sale in Tacoma, Washington, "not to violate American immigration and labor laws by having Dave physically participate."

He never did anything. He was never on the ramp. He never took a bid. But, at one point, he got frustrated with an equipment operator who was bringing a piece of equipment across the ramp. He stepped over and told the operator to "get that thing out of here."[7]

Immigration officials were present at the sale that day, and all they needed to see was Dave Ritchie, a Canadian citizen and not legally allowed to work in the United States, give an order. He was detained and a court date was set. At the same time, Dave was advised to stay out of the country until the case went to trial. Ultimately, the ruling went in Ritchie's favor.

The new partners, or "second founding blood of the company in 1975," with two of the three brothers, including, from left to right, Dave Ritchie (foreground left), Ken Ritchie, Russ Cmolik, Dick Bartel (foreground right), and Bill Gronberg.

"The judge rapped the knuckles of the INS guys for doing what they did, and we got our paperwork [which allows entry to the United States]," Cmolik said.

Changing of the Guard

When John Ritchie left the company, Ritchie Bros. Auctioneers consisted of only about eight or nine people, including Dave Ritchie, Bill Nott, Russ Cmolik, and Dick Bartel in Vancouver, and Ken Ritchie in Kelowna. In Edmonton, the company had Bill Gronberg managing its business.

Bob Carswell, a former Stewart Auctions employee who joined Ritchie Bros. in 1975, remembered working with Ken Ritchie as the company sold equipment from defunct mills. "Everybody knew Ken," Carswell remembered. "They knew how he operated, and everybody was real comfortable with the situation. Ken could just walk through a mill with a piece of paper and in 20 minutes know what it was worth."[8]

Yet Dave Ritchie was still the sole shareholder. In 1975, he made a critical decision to reward the group of employees who had traveled together, bet on one another, and carved out a respectable niche in the auction industry. He sold partnerships to the key employees. The first partners were Dick Bartel with a 20 percent share, Russ Cmolik with a 10 percent share, Ken Ritchie, who maintained a 10 percent stake and ended up leaving the company again in the early 1980s, and Bill Gronberg with 10 percent. Sales that year were $24 million, an increase of more than $2 million over the previous year. In 1978, Stan Koskoska joined as a partner in the Western Canadian region.

These partnerships remained very important. Not only did they reward loyal employees, they spread the wealth of Ritchie Bros. Auctioneers into the group that made it possible.

"I always had profit sharing in the company," said Dave Ritchie. "We always had a system of trying to reward a good salesman and make it work, and I realized that if we were going

to build this company, we were going to need some good people around that were solid citizens and were going to participate on a full scale. So the partnerships gave them a vested interest in what we were doing."[9]

This "vested interest" was important for other reasons as well. In the future, the partnership structure provided a valuable recruiting tool because company officers were able to tell prospective employees that a successful career path at Ritchie Bros. ended up with a partnership in the corporation.

Later, Cmolik would describe this core group as the "second founding blood of the company in 1975, after the three brothers themselves."[10]

The Brink of Disaster

The ink was hardly dry on the partnership agreements, set up through the personal corporations of the newly minted owners, when Ritchie Bros. Auctioneers very nearly went out of business in a single sale. The sale in question was scheduled to take place in Port Orford, Oregon, where the company was looking to sell off the contents of a plywood plant.

"We probably spent two months putting this deal together," said Dick Bartel. "At that time, we didn't really know that particular market, and we had other people tell us the market for this equipment was good although the housing market was down."[11]

Because it was one of the biggest sales attempted in the United States so far and for a kind of equipment Ritchie Bros. wasn't used to dealing with, the company was prompted to do something a little unusual, Cmolik remembered.

"We didn't know anything about plywood," Cmolik said. "We knew about tractors, rolling stock, sawmill equipment, and so on. So we went out and hired two independent appraisers, even independent of each other."[12]

The appraisers assessed the material at $1.5 million, and the auction was set to go forward. Before the auction, however, Ken Ritchie went down to assess the spread and raised the first alert that something might be wrong.

"After a short visit, I realized that the company had made a bad deal and recommended that we not buy David out because of the loss that would develop," Ken said.[13]

Unfortunately, Ken was right about the appraisal. It didn't take long on the day of the auction for the Ritchie team to realize they had made a dreadful mistake. An old boiler that had been appraised at $75,000 went for less than $1,000.[14]

"The first day was a disaster," Bartel said. "At the end of that first day, we knew there was no money to be made. We'd be lucky if we could break even, and we looked really hard at the numbers and said, 'Yeah, we could lose a big chunk of change.' The second day proved our estimates right."[15]

During the devastating bidding, a piece of equipment that stacked and wrapped plywood was auctioned off for $6,500 to an absentee bidder. Right after the sale was announced, however, a buyer came running toward the podium and announced that he had actually made a bid of $14,000 and the equipment was rightfully his since he had the higher bid. Cmolik later told what happened:

Dave was there, and he looked at the clerk and said, "Who bought it?" The clerk announced that the name of the absentee bidder was in fact the gentleman who was demanding that he was the legal buyer. Dave turned to the man and, despite the fact that he knew that Ritchie Bros. was on the point of insolvency, said, "Well, you already bought it for $6,500."[16]

Even had Ritchie insisted on the higher price, it wouldn't have made much difference. At the end of the sale, Ritchie Bros. had lost $600,000, an amount great enough to seriously threaten the young partnership. Dave Ritchie, who had just sold shares of the company to his brother and closest friends, felt terrible about the disaster. "They were all sick with it," he said. "I said, 'Hey, if you don't want the stock, I'll give you your money back.' Not one of them took it."[17]

The Surrey auction yard was located on the Fraser River and next to the Pattullo Bridge. Ritchie Bros. added permanent yards throughout the 1970s.

now 375, 75, 75, I have 350, need 75, 75, 75, try 360... 360, thank you, now 370, 370, 370, three hundred and seventy thousand

50   THE LEGEND OF RITCHIE BROS. AUCTIONEERS

Instead, the partners went to their banker, Al Perley of the Royal Bank in Vancouver. Perley was a longtime banking partner of Ritchie Bros. and knew the company well. In fact, he personally had supported the company through so much that at one point a younger Dave Ritchie thought Perley owned the Royal Bank. This time, however, they had to approach Perley with bad news.

"I walked right in and told him flat out what had happened," Dave said. "We had lost half a million or a little more. He said, 'OK, Dave,' and I was so pleased that he had that faith and wasn't jumping off a bridge, as some bankers would. I made up my mind that by the end of that year, we would have made it all back and then some."[18]

And they did. By the end of the year, the company had made up the loss.

"That was one of the times when Dave showed his leadership and said, 'We're going to carry on and grow this thing,'" remembered Malcolm Clay, an accountant with KPMG who worked with Ritchie Bros. "This was a big loss for a new business, and there were some of them that said, 'Well, let's just retreat into Canada and carry on making our money up here and abandon this idea of expanding into the U.S.' It was a turning point for the company."[19]

Incidentally, at about the same time this sale took place, John Ritchie returned from South Africa and back to the family company. His tenure this time, however, would be short lived. Just prior to an auction at which John was supposed to be calling bids, he quit unexpectedly. Fortunately, another auctioneer was found, and the sale went off without a hitch.[20]

Investing in Land

Ritchie Bros. would not be ruined by an individual sale. At the time, the company rented a single permanent auction yard in Vancouver. This 10-acre site was situated under the Pattullo Bridge across the Fraser River and was sometimes called "the supermarket of heavy industrial equipment sales."[21] There the company hosted six auctions that grossed approximately $6 million per year. On average, each auction sold about 350 items to an audience of 700.

At the time, all of Ritchie's auctions, including the regular sales in Edmonton, were staged on leased or rented land. This presented a set of challenges all its own as the Ritchie team struggled to make an auction site as comfortable and inviting as possible, knowing the site would have to be vacated in a short time.

In 1976, Ritchie Bros. took a major step with the purchase of property at the Nisku Industrial Park, located in Edmonton, Alberta. It was the first permanent Ritchie Bros. auction yard, and Edmonton was a logical place. The area was home to a large sales office under Bill Gronberg and had already been the site of Ritchie Bros.' largest single sale to date.

dollars... Anyone at 370? 370 YES! Now 380, now 390, 390, 90, 90, 90, one more time, sir? At three hundred and ninety thousand...

CHAPTER FOUR: CHANGING OF THE GUARD   51

"Instead of having our manpower out trying to find a yard to conduct an auction in, then build infrastructure and tear it apart and move, we wanted the same place to go to all the time," Russ Cmolik said of Nisku. "Our manpower would be able to focus on the business and not worry about where the yard was. Also, it would give us a presence in the community, so it would be easier to attract quality staff."[22]

Even though he was in favor of a permanent site, Cmolik remembered his reaction when he found out that Dave Ritchie wanted to open in Nisku.

We were in Edmonton, Alberta, and the snow was blowing, and Dave sees a building that has no floor. A company had begun

building it with offices in the front and a shop in the back, but there were economic issues in 1975 and it was empty. In all, it had 25,000 square feet, and Dave wanted to buy it. I was sitting there saying, "You're crazy, that is too much money. It has no floor in it. If we buy it, we have to put a bunch of money into it."[23]

Nevertheless, Ritchie soon closed the deal. Shortly afterward, the company issued a press release proclaiming:

In 1976, the company opened the Nisku Industrial Park location to house the headquarters of their Prairie Division. Under Company Director and Prairie Manager Bill Gronberg, the permanent staff handles all sales transactions in the Prairie Provinces, as well as giving support to Ritchie Bros. representatives located in Calgary and Winnipeg.

The fully fenced 18.5 acre location is one of the finest auction sites in North America. The 15,000-square-foot buildings are ultra modern and air conditioned throughout.[24]

Like any community receiving new business, Edmonton was pleased when the auctioneer located there. Although Ritchie Bros. didn't employ hundreds of local residents, the company was nonetheless important to local economies. The auctions brought in hundreds of travelers from all over the world. These buyers needed hotels and restaurants. In addition, Ritchie's presence brought needed revenue to local catering companies, security companies, transportation companies that moved the equipment, finance companies, and many other local businesses.

Roland Russell, founder of El-Russ Equipment in Calgary, visited the Nisku site shortly after it opened. "It was like a military

In 1976, Ritchie Bros. purchased land at the Nisku Industrial Park in Edmonton and opened the largest permanent industrial auction yard in Canada. It was the company's flagship site for years to come.

390, 90, 90, 90, and I have... FOUR HUNDRED, just in time, sir, 400, four hundred thousand, 400, 410, 410, 410, now 420, 420...

52 THE LEGEND OF RITCHIE BROS. AUCTIONEERS

operation," he remembered. "Everything was neat and tidy."[25]

By the end of the decade, Ritchie purchased and opened two other permanent yards, one at Surrey, outside of Vancouver, and another at Kamloops, in British Columbia. Together these two yards accounted for approximately 90 percent of all heavy industrial auctioneering in the province.

"The amount of business in an area once we opened up a yard went up 50 percent," Cmolik said. "So that became a fundamental way by which the company was going to move forward."[26]

The Consummate Auctioneer

By this time, Dave stuck to a pattern that would become familiar throughout the years. He traveled relentlessly and attended every auction possible. While at the auctions, Dave was deeply involved in the operating details and

Above: Cleaning, sandblasting, and painting were standard preauction features of Ritchie Bros. sales.

Below: Before a sale, customers were invited to walk the grounds, where they would find dozers with their blades perfectly aligned and cranes angled uniformly and neatly. Every attention was paid to presentation.

Jim. are you there at 420? Four hundred and twenty thousand... SOLD to Larry's man for four hundred and ten thousand.

CHAPTER FOUR: CHANGING OF THE GUARD   53

highly visible. "He has probably shaken more hands than any politician alive," remarked Bill Bremmeyer, owner of Bremmeyer Logging Company and Bremmeyer Equipment, both in Ravensdale, Washington. "He's also got a memory for people's names that's almost more than you can believe. He'll meet people after years and remember their wives' and kids' names."[27]

Dave also maintained the parties for which Ritchie Bros. had become famous. He operated the company with the enthusiasm of someone who loves what he is doing, and this attitude spread to other employees. Customer after customer would remark on the enthusiasm and integrity of Ritchie Bros. employees—even if they were talking about a high-stakes poker game. But Dave was always in it for the fun, and when the parties or gambling looked like they might get out of hand, he moved to bring things under control. Friends remember one poker game when a player got carried away and lost more than he could afford. Without drawing attention to it, Dave later returned the man's money.

This spirit of generosity extended even to the auctions. At one particular sale in Prince George, a young man was bidding on an all-terrain vehicle. It soon became apparent to Dave, however, that the young man was mentally handicapped. Dave stopped the bidding and asked over the loudspeaker system where the young man's father was. The father soon appeared, and Dave asked if his son could handle the machine. Naturally, the father assumed he meant financially, so he responded, "No, we can't afford this thing. Absolutely not."

"No," Dave said, "that's not what I'm asking. Can he operate it safely?"

The father said sure, his son could operate the machine. When the sale began again, Dave himself bid on the machine and purchased it, then gave the young man his vehicle.[28]

The patterns set long ago at Scout Hall in Kelowna had by now become tradition. Dave was an indefatigable worker, dividing his time at the auctions between talking to people and shaking hands and standing up catching bids. He would often be the first to arrive at an auction site and still be working there long after the last piece of equipment had rolled across the ramp.

"Everybody knows Dave Ritchie," said Dick Bartel. "These guys would come to the sale, and if they have a problem, the first guy they go to is Dave. He's approachable."[29]

The auctions themselves had also fully developed their trademark feel by this time. Regular attendees expected to see the equipment clean, orderly, and painted, and the buildings swept. Before a sale, the heavy equipment would be neatly lined up, dozer blades angled identically, trucks parked in a perfect line, and crane arms arched into a tunnel of yellow. This attention to detail came from Dave Ritchie himself; many people remember seeing him stop and direct a truck to be rolled back a couple inches or a smudge to be wiped from an otherwise clean piece of equipment.

"He had his finger on everything that happened," Cmolik said. "He knew every yard man and what they were doing, where they were deployed. He knew every brochure. Dave had a personal interest in what was going on."[30]

Roundup

Dave might have had a personal interest, but Ritchie Bros. was growing, making it more difficult to keep open lines of communication throughout the company. This was exacerbated by the geographical reach of the com-

In summer 1977, Ritchie Bros. sold off the entire contents of the Texada Island mine, located on Texada Island, just north of Vancouver. The sale included not only equipment but the entire contents of the town, including buildings and material.

CHAPTER FOUR: CHANGING OF THE GUARD   55

pany. Between Canada and the United States, Ritchie Bros. was active across several thousand miles.

With this in mind, the decision was made in 1977 to publish a company newsletter called *Roundup*. The publication was designed to "bring you a comprehensive view of who's who, what's what and possibly why, across the miles that separate these little bands of outposts...these rugged pioneers, this far-flung empire...these men and women of Ritchie Bros. Auctioneers."[31]

In addition to vignettes about Ritchie Bros. staff and auctions, the magazine also had small news items concerning the company. One of the first issues, dated July 12, 1977, had an article about an auction in Surrey that was televised by CHAN-TV in Vancouver. This broadcast was probably one of the first documentaries of an industrial auction in progress, and four

minutes were devoted exclusively to Wayne Clark, a colorful auctioneer.

The same issue also noted that Dave Ritchie has "purchased himself a 53-foot yacht to transport prospective clients to the Texada mine site."[32]

Texada Island Mine

This last item was of no small interest—not because of the yacht but because of the sale it concerned. Ritchie Bros. had landed a contract to auction equipment associated with the mine on Texada Island.

Texada Island lay about 50 miles north of Vancouver in the Georgia Strait. It was discovered and named by Spanish explorer Jose Maria Narvaez in 1791. Almost a century later, a fisherman named Harry Trim discovered iron-ore deposits on the island and filed a mineral claim. In 1897, New York industrialist Harry Whitney Treat set up the Vananda Copper and Gold Company and opened three mines. Within a few years, the island had a population of 3,000 miners and related businesspeople.

Before the big equipment was sold, Ritchie Bros. held smaller-lot sales of tools and related equipment.

twenty-seven-five, seven-five, and 30, 30, 30, now 31, 31, 32, 32, 32, Don, does your man want it? I need 32... thirty-two thousand, 32, 32,

56   THE LEGEND OF RITCHIE BROS. AUCTIONEERS

The Texada Island mine, which Ritchie Bros. was preparing to auction off, opened in 1952. In its short life, this successful mine shipped out 11 million tons of iron concentrate and 100,000 tons of copper concentrate, in addition to small amounts of silver and gold. By the 1970s, however, the Canadian iron ore mines were losing a competitive race with open-pit iron mines in Australia and were forced to close down. "They don't allow mining companies to leave ghost towns behind anymore," mine manager A. M. Walker told a local newspaper when word of the sale was announced.[33]

Since the Canadian government no longer allowed ghost towns, Ritchie Bros. found itself auctioning off a small city, using Dave Ritchie's personal boats to ferry people out to the deserted mining town. "We caught a nice big salmon and got some oysters ourselves," he remembered.

And when I was walking through town, I spied a lady who had a very good garden, so I asked her what she'd take for a nice feed of vegetables. I paid her quite a price, I think at that time about $50 or $100 for peas and carrots and beets. It was all really first class. I had a niece that did the cooking for us on the boat and had one of the greatest feeds. We had so many guys, they had to eat in shifts because we didn't have enough dishes. But we could make the food good, and the customers who were on that trip will never forget it.[34]

That same year, Frank McFadden joined the company during a summer break from college and was sent up to Texada Island to help the auction. "It was the dirtiest thing you could ever imagine," McFadden later said. "There was 25 years of debris everywhere. So we bought it, and we had to make sure every closet and shop was emptied and things are organized and inventoried. I was rust from head to toe every night."[35]

The Texada Island mine sale was finally staged on August 25, 1977. The wide variety of mining equipment up for sale included jaw crushers, cone crushers, trucks, loaders, shovels, dozers, drills, and ore carriers. McFadden, who had been hired specifically to help with the sale during a summer off from college, never returned to school and signed on with the company instead.

Although "It was a great sale and included some really nice antique stuff," sale prices tended to be about 25 percent below what was hoped for. Buyers' enthusiasm was dampened by the cost of removing buildings and equipment from the steeply sloping site and the trouble of removing the equipment by water.[36]

Heavy Equipment Auctions Come of Age

In the mid- to late 1970s, it was becoming increasingly obvious that the years of work at Ritchie Bros. were beginning to pay off. Although auctions had existed long before Ritchie Bros. was founded, many outside observers credit Ritchie Bros. with pioneering the modern form of industrial auction. The company had successfully turned auctions from slightly seedy affairs in which everybody benefited except the actual buyer into a legitimate, honorable business with strict rules of ethical conduct. Proof of this transformation could be seen in the grandstand at almost any Ritchie Bros. auction. At first, the sales were heavily attended by used equipment dealers, and the auction business was basically a wholesale venture. Throughout the years, however, more and more end users began to attend Ritchie Bros. auctions, and the company earned credit for turning industrial auctioneering into a viable retail business.

Opposite: Dave Ritchie, pictured in the 1970s. As Ritchie Bros. added new permanent yards and continued its push across Canada and into the United States, Ritchie began to envision the day when the company would go worldwide.

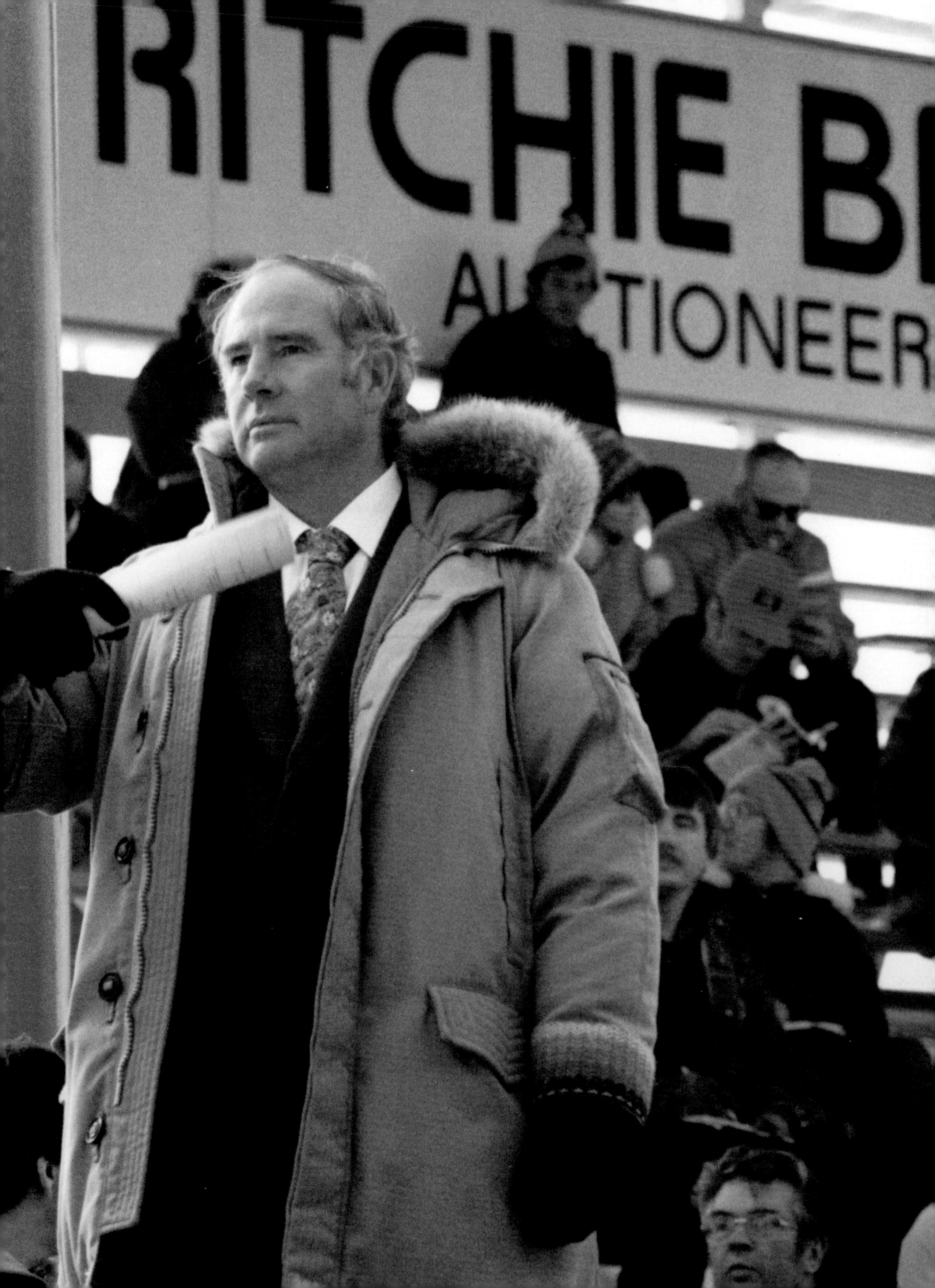
RITCHIE B

32, Johnny's in the lead at 31. I need 32 from your man, Don... 32, YES! Now 33, 33, 33, now 34 to you, Don, 34, 34, 34, are you there,

58   THE LEGEND OF RITCHIE BROS. AUCTIONEERS

At the same time, the prices fetched by equipment at auction were rising. Ritchie Bros. maintained a reputation for holding fair and honest auctions that featured strong marketing efforts to attract qualified buyers. Before any sale, the company put together a series of brochures advertising what was available and placed advertisements in trade journals and magazines promoting the sale. In addition, the company maintained a database of frequent customers, who were mailed auction brochures. By the late 1970s, Ritchie Bros. was printing and mailing thousands and thousands of brochures for each of its auctions.

As Ritchie Bros. effected its transformation of the auction business, new issues began to emerge. Used-equipment dealers, who were still attendees and customers at Ritchie's auctions, began to worry that perhaps this young auction company would put them out of business. After all, many consignors liked Ritchie's fast conversion of equipment into cash and, for almost

inexplicable reasons, a certain segment of the buying population seemed to prefer buying at auction. Some dealers reported instances in which a customer was considering a purchase of warranted used equipment but hesitated—and then attended an auction soon after and bought a similar piece of equipment, which had no warranty at all.

Ritchie Bros., however, had no intention of competing with traditional used-equipment dealers. In fact, the company considered these people customers and close friends. Nevertheless, Ritchie Bros. continued to grow and spread its increasingly complex operation throughout North America.

Used equipment didn't always reach the auctioneer in the best condition—these particular dozers had to be dragged from mud. To make hard-used equipment more salable, Ritchie Bros. offered sandblasting and painting services.

Don? Thirty-four thousand, 34, 34, 34, last chance at thirty-four thousand... and the trailer is... SOLD!

CHAPTER FOUR: CHANGING OF THE GUARD   59

In 1977, computer specialist Ken Dunn was hired to install a computer system that could handle extensive mailing lists and appraisals, in addition to the routine tasks of accounting.[37]

The computer, at a cost of $10,000, was a valuable addition to the Ritchie Bros. appraisal function. It was soon programmed with an extensive database of records gleaned from the sales figures of seven auction houses, including Ritchie Bros. When queried, it could display the sale price of any particular piece of equipment sold at a given time.

The Growth Cycles

Nearing the last part of the 1970s, Ritchie Bros. had changed dramatically in just a few years. One of the founding brothers had left, and new partners had been brought in. It had opened new remote auction sites and had cemented its reputation as a leading industrial auction company. Sales in 1977 reached $47 million—up from only $1 million in 1963. In those 14 years, Ritchie Bros. had staged 287 auctions, selling off all manner of construction, forestry, and mining equipment, and had grown beyond the original home base of Kelowna into Richmond, Toronto, Montreal, Edmonton,

Calgary, Winnipeg, Prince George, Kamloops, and Surrey. The company had several permanent auction sites; the yards in Surrey and Kamloops had been upgraded to the level of the Nisku site. Finally, the company had an American subsidiary based in Portland, Oregon.

All of this growth had begun to attract attention outside the cloistered world of industrial equipment sales. Ritchie Bros. began to receive coverage in local newspapers and on television. In 1977, an article in *Roundup* estimated how much free publicity Ritchie Bros. was receiving.

It would be in the hundred thousand dollar plus mark; when you consider that the CBC charges $16,000 a minute for network coverage; that most magazines run over $1,000 per page and that newspapers can range from a low of $500 to a high of $5,000, you can see that our publicity runs into big money.[38]

As 1977 drew to a close, a spokesman for Finning Tractor Ltd., British Columbia's Caterpillar franchisee and also a large used-equipment dealer, remarked, "On a scale of ten, I rate Ritchie nine to ten when it comes to knowing what they are doing."[39]

Stuart Island, pictured in the 1990s. Dave Ritchie bought land on Stuart Island in the 1970s.

CHAPTER FIVE

THE TRAVELING SHOW

1977–1979

Our business is good when business is good, and our business is better when business is tough.

—Dave Ritchie

FOR AN INDUSTRIAL auction company, nothing is sweeter than the announcement that a major construction job is about to get underway. Ritchie Bros.' first big industrial equipment sale was connected to the huge Trans-Canada Highway, and many of its subsequent big sales were likewise related to huge construction undertakings. As the company grew, Ritchie Bros. was in a position to pursue larger and larger spreads—often bidding on equipment used in the most ambitious undertakings in Canada.

In a lot of cases, the effort to sell a project began years before the final yard of concrete was poured. "We liked to get in on those huge projects three or four years before they were done," said Bob Carswell, who worked in Calgary and Western Canada. "Our eyes light up when we hear about big projects because there's a potential customer there."[1]

The late 1970s saw several major roadway and pipeline construction ventures as companies prepared for an economic turnaround. This activity translated into future opportunity for Ritchie Bros. In 1977, Ritchie Bros. conducted 37 auctions, mostly in Western Canada, and grossed nearly $47 million. A year later,

gross sales rose to almost $65 million.

Although Ritchie Bros. still lacked a major presence in the United States, it was gaining exposure among American buyers, partly due to favorable trade regulations between the United States and Canada. According to U.S. law, American-made products sold outside the country were free from import duty when reentering the United States. This favorable situation was aided by the declining value of the Canadian dollar, which meant that savvy American buyers could purchase equipment in Canada and import it duty free back home.

A barrier to U.S./Canadian trade remained, however, remembered Gary Caufield, controller for Ritchie Bros. The two countries had different transportation, safety, and environmental standards, and equipment that was bought in Canada was sometimes held up at the border.[2]

Ritchie Bros.' marketing campaigns, auction brochures, and reputation for selling good equipment at unreserved auctions transformed the auction industry.

But this problem wasn't serious, and Ritchie Bros. continued to enjoy rising sales. During weaker economies, when contractors and industry scaled back, the company was more likely to purchase equipment outright rather than contract for percentage commission sales. In this way, the company could capitalize on the spiraling costs of new equipment, which created a great incentive for customers to buy used equipment.

"Inflation is causing a tremendous demand for used equipment," said Dick Bartel. "Our buyers and sellers both benefit. The seller will probably realize from 60 to 70 percent of his original investment, and the buyer will be buying equipment at probably half the price if he bought new. It makes sense to consider the auction route."[3]

The Great Sales

Ritchie Bros.' history is unique in many ways. Rather than a story of manufacturing firsts or technological innovation, Ritchie's heritage is a collection of stories from auctions—each hopefully bigger than the last, but each different and each a part of the Ritchie story. In 1977, Ritchie Bros. scored with a sale for Royal Paving in Manitoba. It took Russ Cmolik a month to negotiate the deal to buy the company's shares, working in winter temperatures that plummeted to 40 degrees below zero Fahrenheit. The sale was conducted that spring.

That same year, Ritchie Bros. put together a sale for the Mica Dam hydroelectric project in the interior of British Columbia. Beth Farrell, the same Ritchie Bros. veteran who helicoptered money back from the La Grande Riviére project, worked on that deal and returned home with a cat named Mica. The job was interesting because it was a heavily unionized effort, which made it more challenging because Ritchie had to work within union rules to conduct the sale.

The following year, the company held the largest one-day auction in Canadian history when it grossed about $5 million at a sale in Red Deer, Alberta. A week later, the company broke the Canadian West Coast record with a sale of $3 million at Surrey, British Columbia.

Perhaps no sale stands out in the company's collective memory of those waning years of the 1970s like a Ritchie Bros. mine sale in the Yukon. At the time, Canadian mining techniques and regulation were changing. For decades, miners had extracted gold, silver, coal, lead, zinc, copper, and other minerals from the earth. When one high-grade mine was depleted, the mining company simply closed down the shaft and moved to another, more productive site. In many cases, when a mine closed down, the small town that had sprung up around it was also abandoned, and soon the countryside was dotted with frontier ghost towns at old mining sites. By the late 1970s, however, mining was shifting to open-pit operations, and the Canadian government had decreed that the land around closed mines had to be completely cleared and allowed to revert to its natural state.

So when the Cassiar Asbestos Corporation decided to close up its operation at Clinton Creek, it had to dispose of the contents of the entire corporate town around the mine. It was a small price to pay. Over its 11-year history at the mine, Cassiar Asbestos had removed $275 million worth of ore. Although Ritchie Bros. had already sold off the contents of a mining town at Texada, the Cassiar Asbestos mine presented a different challenge: Clinton Creek was located about 60 miles from the fabled mining town of Dawson City in the heart of the frozen and forbidding Yukon Territory.

"I went up there with Ken Ritchie," remembered Frank McFadden, who had also helped at the Texada mine site. "We basically contracted for the entire town site and everything in it. It was a gorgeous spot."[4]

To get the word out, the company produced thousands of auction brochures for mass mailings. A total of 558 registered bidders soon signed up to attend the two-day auction: day one at Whitehorse, which was a two-hour flight from Dawson City, and day two at the mine site itself in Clinton Creek. To get people to the site,

thousand, OK I'll do 75, 75, 75, now 80, 80, now 85, 85, 85 and 90, 90 thousand, 90, 90, 90. Dave, does your man want one

CHAPTER FIVE: THE TRAVELING SHOW   63

In 1978, Ritchie Bros. Auctioneers contracted to sell all of the contents of the 100-year-old Phoenix mine. Shown in 1919 (the mine in the background), Phoenix had produced copper and gold until being converted into an open-pit mine in the 1950s.

Dave Ritchie chartered various aircraft to fly between Whitehorse and Clinton Creek.

The first day's sale went well, and the buyers began leaving in shifts to attend the second part of the sale in Clinton Creek. The shuttle flights went smoothly right up until darkness descended. Most of the buyers had reached the mine site safely, but the Ritchie Bros. staff was still in Whitehorse and the plane was not equipped to fly at night!

This problem was soon solved on the ground. The Ritchie Bros. team contracted a bus to make the eight-hour drive at night along an all-weather gravel road. The bus departed Whitehorse around 10 P.M. and arrived in Clinton Creek early the next morning. The auction began only a couple hours later—on time!

By the time the final gavel fell, the sale had grossed more than $2.5 million. It was not a huge number by Ritchie standards, but a success considering the location.

At the same time, many of the buyers were pleased with the incredible bargains available. A Dawson City man, for example, walked away with the Malamute Saloon and Lounge for only $800. Several homes were sold, both three- and four-bedroom, for between $2,000 and $5,000. The town's curling rink and ice arena sold for $8,500. The most unusual purchase was probably made by Znidar Bros. of Ontario, which purchased an entire aerial tramway system for $15,000. The biggest transportation headache probably belonged to the Albertan who paid $50,000 for an 11,800-square-foot Dryer building for use in his rock-crushing operation.

"The whole place was sold and now that site is flat," McFadden said. "You wouldn't know that there was ever a town there. Most of the transportation was accomplished by moving everything to Alaska and shipping it from there. Or it came down to Dawson City and down the Yukon River."[5]

Around the same time, Ritchie Bros. landed another mine deal, this time concerning the Phoenix mine in southern British Columbia. This mine was first opened in 1857 by pioneers seeking copper and gold; then between 1899 and 1919 it was worked as an underground copper mine. During its heyday,

more shot? He's been with us all the way... 90 thousand, 90 thousand, last chance... and... now 95, 95, now 100, 100 thousand

64   THE LEGEND OF RITCHIE BROS. AUCTIONEERS

the small mountain town boasted 3,000 residents, served by 17 saloons. In 1919, however, the worldwide demand for copper dropped and the mine was closed. It was reopened in 1945 after World War II, then bought by the Granby Mining Corporation in 1958 and changed to an open-pit mine.

Interestingly, while cleaning and preparing the equipment for auction, the Granby Mining Corporation recovered more than 250 ounces of gold from the old machinery. The sale took place on October 31, 1978.

To Stuart Island and Richmond

Ritchie Bros., then almost 20 years old, still retained a close-knit, family-like culture. In 1978, Dick Bartel was named president of Ritchie Bros. "I didn't want the job at all," he remembered. "I was quite happy doing what I was doing, but it worked out. We did everything by the committee of Russ Cmolik, Dave Ritchie, myself, and Bob Carswell. We would more or less work things out together that way."[6]

Indeed. Formal titles were often eschewed in favor of job descriptions. It was hard to even say that Dick Bartel was named president in 1978—looking back 20 years later, people would describe his title in 1978 as anything from president to general manager to chief operating officer to director. What mattered more was results. Mike Ritchie recalled getting a phone call that year from Bartel regarding a potential sale.

"I was living in Toronto at the time," Mike said.

Dick had a call from a trustee and was informed that a construction company in Edmundston, New Brunswick, Dube Construction, had to sell their equipment. Dick asked me to get on the next flight out as the tenders were due the next day at noon. After flying to Fredricton and renting a car there, I arrived only about two hours before the tenders were due. I reviewed the assets, called Dick, and prepared our cash offer, and had it to the trustee just in time. He opened the tenders right away, and we were high bidder by $100,000. I began to think I made an error in my quick appraisal and worried until the day of the sale. We ended up making a very good commission.[7]

Dave Ritchie had these decorative plates made after memorable fishing experiences. The plate on the left shows a particularly good day on the water that yielded a bounty of Pacific salmon. The plate at right shows a salmon with marauding dogfish still attached to its belly.

CHAPTER FIVE: THE TRAVELING SHOW

One thing that hadn't changed was Dave Ritchie's passion for fun. In the late 1970s, he bought land on Stuart Island, just north of Vancouver and not far from British Columbia's fabled Campbell River. Here the lifelong fishing enthusiast began to develop a Ritchie Bros. fishing camp. The camp was managed by Tammy Ritchie, Dave's daughter, who would host groups there for the next 20 years.

"It started out with about 20 acres," Tammy said in 1999. "Then he built a barge, which got written up in an international yachting magazine when it was first built. Every week, I see a different group of 10 or 12 guys, usually Ritchie Bros. customers and salespeople. It creates a lot of good business, a lot of good contacts, and a lot of good memories. Even when people don't catch fish, they see eagles or whales."[8]

Yet fishing and card playing were the main draws. As the years went by, Ritchie Bros. hired guides to take customers fishing, and it wasn't uncommon to have people land 25- or 30-pound Pacific salmon. The stories from these fishing trips are legion, and all of the visitors to Stuart Island cherish and repeat them. Pacific salmon are a world-class sport fish renowned for aerial acrobatics and sheer power. When the big fish get up next to a boat, they are known to

Above and inset: The Stuart Island camp was equipped with many luxuries, including a yacht for guests, later replaced by a barge. Because of the island's remote location, moving guests around by sea plane was most efficient.

turn and run back for the open water—sometimes adding to the challenge by attracting voracious dogfish (actually a member of the shark family) that can rip the trophy apart before it can be landed.

Like the old hall in Kelowna, Stuart Island gave Ritchie and his friends, employees, and customers a place to play. Sometimes big yachts would pull up to the remote island and a card game would begin that went uninterrupted for the weekend. The fish were safe at these times. Once a gentleman flew up from Texas and insisted he wanted to play dominoes, so Ritchie bought dominoes and the Texan taught everybody how to play.

With relatively few employees, Ritchie Bros. was a great place to work and socialize. Gary Caufield, who joined in 1978 as corporate controller from KPMG, remembered the transition from the big accounting house to the smaller, private auctioneer.

"We were a small company, so if we lost $5,000, that was a lot of money," Caufield remembered. "We did almost everything ourselves and never used a lot of outside help like lawyers and accountants. When I started as corporate controller, we had only a small presence in the United States and most of our business was in Western Canada. Edmonton was our most successful yard, plus good yards in Surrey and Kamloops and a new yard in Prince George."[9]

Caufield, with a staff of only about seven, ran the largest corporate department in Ritchie Bros. The accounting staff consisted of two

Ritchie Bros. was a close-knit company whose reputation was built on the character of the people running it, including, from left to right standing, Bill Gronberg, Russ Cmolik, Stan Koskoska, and Ken Ritchie; seated left to right are Dave Ritchie and Dick Bartel.

Wrap 'em up, put a bow on 'em and they're gone, gone forever—he took them all!

CHAPTER FIVE: THE TRAVELING SHOW   67

field accountants, one paralegal secretary, an accounts payable clerk, and three head office accountants. Typically, the field accountants traveled to a remote site before the sale and located a field office, hired temporary help, obtained transfer documents, had telephones installed, arranged for catering firms, and ensured that transportation and finance companies would both be on-site during the day of the sale. Since a lot of equipment was taken into the United States, customs brokers were also invited to be part of the proceedings.

Every item purchased had to be paid for within seven days of the purchase. Consignors were paid less than 20 days after the sale. Over the years, Ritchie Bros. had become so efficient at conducting auctions and arranging financing that bad debts in 1979 amounted to less than $25,000 on revenues of $66 million. As Bartel later remarked, "We'll be happy to put anything on the auction block except one thing. The best auctioneering staff in Canada."[10]

Although still small, by 1979 Ritchie Bros. had finally outgrown its headquarters in Vancouver. To accommodate future growth, the company expanded its corporate administrative building in Richmond. The day Ritchie Bros. moved into its new building, a congratulatory telegram arrived from Nebraska auctioneer Forke Brothers.

This telegram from Forke Brothers was an interesting development. Sent in the spirit of friendly competition, it was nonetheless evidence that Forke, which also had an excellent reputation for honesty and integrity, wasn't too worried about losing its position as the world's largest auctioneer of heavy industrial equipment. At least not to a young Canadian company that was hardly established in the United States.

To careful observers, however, Forke's lead wasn't so secure. Although both companies were auctioneers and both believed that auctions were a good way to sell used equipment, there were major differences in the way Forke Brothers and Ritchie Bros. operated. Like most auction companies, Forke was a more hands-off operation.

"If you had equipment to sell, Forke would go in and say, 'Here's what you have to do.' Then they would send in the auctioneers and the clerks and so on," Caufield remembered. "They would perform a service for you, and then it would be your job to prepare the equipment and lay out the yard. Ritchie Bros., on the other hand, was a turnkey operation. You signed a contract and you paid a commission. The rest was our responsibility."[11]

And Ritchie took this responsibility seriously. Its yards were designed with comfort in mind, and the events were totally professional. Also, Dave Ritchie continued to attend as many auctions as possible, still maintaining his ambitious, year-round travel schedule.

In 1979, when the new headquarters was finished, *Roundup* covered the opening:

After five months of dust, dirt, noise and inconvenience, our crammed house-headquarters of old has been transformed into a handsome 8,000-square-foot building. The original terms of reference concerning the new building were these: it must be reasonably priced, attractive, and functional as well as to incorporate as much of the existing building as possible. [The company] has succeeded in the attractive brown brick structure.[12]

A minor crisis during the construction signaled the company's growing needs. To consolidate records storage, all the filing cabinets were moved into a single room. Each cabinet weighed about 1,200 pounds, meaning that together, Ritchie Bros. placed almost six tons of paper in the room. This demand was simply more than the ordinary 2x8 wooden floor joists could handle. The morning after the filing room was stocked, workers arrived to see the floor visibly sagging under the weight of Ritchie's business.

The floor was hastily reinforced, and "A secretary who continued working throughout was duly recommended for the Victoria Cross."[13]

By the 1980s, Ritchie Bros. Auctioneers was firmly established throughout Canada and the United States. Each of these auction brochures covered a single sale.

CHAPTER SIX

COMING OF AGE

1980–1986

I want to be the greatest auctioneer of all time.

—Pre-eminent Ritchie Bros. auctioneer
Wayne "Digger" Yoos, early 1980s

*Then you have to come to work for
the greatest auction company in the world!*

—Dave Ritchie's response

THE 1980s BEGAN WELL FOR Ritchie Bros. and bad for just about everybody else. For the second time in 10 years, a serious recession swept through the construction business as interest rates in Canada and the United States skyrocketed. At one point, interest rates in the United States hovered between 17 percent and 18 percent.

Not only did major equipment manufacturers suffer; contractors and equipment brokers were also hit hard. But as was the case during the recession of the early 1970s, the news wasn't terrible for Ritchie Bros. The company specialized in rapid turnover of used equipment and was in a position to help ailing customers raise cash quickly.

One such customer was Terry Simpson, owner of Pacific Forklift in Surrey, British Columbia. In 1982, Simpson's company owed almost $1 million at an interest rate of more than 20 percent. "Ritchie Bros. did a major sale for us that really pulled us out of the glue," Simpson remembered. "We sold 98 forklifts in a single day, and Ritchie Bros. really got us away from our debt."[1]

This ability to help customers and thrive during recessionary times was an important factor in the company's growth.

"The industrial equipment auction business is relatively insulated from cyclical economic trends," stated a company prospectus. "In many cases economic fluctuations or downturns can lead to increased levels of used equipment for consignment, and greater demand for used, rather than new, equipment."[2]

In 1981, Ritchie Bros. recorded sales of $99 million. A year later, sales had jumped to $131 million. The increase wasn't due only to recession-driven business. Ritchie Bros. continued seeking out larger contracts for used equipment, always looking for contracts associated with tremendous undertakings. Beginning in the 1960s, British Columbia entered an era of mega construction projects as the Canadian government sought ways to

Throughout the first half of the 1980s, Ritchie Bros. continued its aggressive expansion, pursuing yellow iron throughout North America and around the world.

it'll get there, 100, 1... 1... 100 thousand! Let's go with 70, 70, 70 thousand... 70... 70... 7... 7... 7... 70, c'mon gentlemen,

70   THE LEGEND OF RITCHIE BROS. AUCTIONEERS

Ritchie Bros. continued to invite more partners into the company, awarding partnerships to employees who distinguished themselves and helped move the company into new areas. These included (from left) Marvin Chantler, Ed Banser, and Roger Rummel, who all became partners in the 1980s.

harness the region's enormous hydroelectric power potential. The government proposed various schemes to harness the power of entire river systems, and several of these tremendous, long-term projects were launched.

Years later, one such project, a huge dam on the Peace River in northeastern British Columbia, was finally nearing completion. This dam, named the W. A. C. Bennett dam, diminished the flow of the 380-mile Peace River and created the largest man-made lake in North America, Williston Lake. When the project was done, Ritchie Bros. was contracted to auction off the equipment. In September 1980, more than 1,400 registered bidders poured into the remote hamlet of Hudson Hope, located 56 miles west of the Alaska Highway, hoping for a bargain.[3]

For that particular sale, however, few bargains were to be had because of a high level of demand for used equipment. Ritchie auctioned off 1,263 lots to buyers who had traveled from all over Canada, the United States, and Japan. At the end of the day, the sale grossed $5 million. Most of the equipment, remembered Russ Cmolik, went to Canadian contractors because high prices forced out used-equipment dealers, unable to turn a profit on expensive machines bought at auction.[4]

The Roster Grows

The early part of the decade was important for other reasons besides the big sales. In 1980, Ken Ritchie again retired from the company (this time permanently), and two new partners were accepted.

One of the new partners, Marvin Chantler, Eastern Canada sales manager and partner, had joined the company in 1979. His responsibilities included managing the inspections, appraisals, and sales of industrial and construction equipment throughout Eastern Canada, Ontario, Quebec, and the Maritimes.

The second new partner was Ed Banser, now the U.S. region's manager. Banser had joined Ritchie Bros. in 1972 as a yardman in Edmonton, moving to Prince George in 1975, where he established Ritchie Bros.' business in the region. In 1980, the same year he was made a partner, Ritchie Bros. was strong enough in Prince George to open up a permanent auction yard. Banser remembered the challenge:

When I went to Prince George, the company said, "Go. Prove to us that you can do the job. If you can prove to us that you can do the job, we'll talk about an increase in salary."

Above: Ken Ritchie catching bids at a Ritchie Bros. auction in 1982

Below: The Ritchie Bros. group during one of the company's conventions in Palm Springs in the early 1980s. These gatherings allowed Ritchie Bros. to collect everybody in one spot, a rare occurrence in the far-flung company.

Nothing happened for a while, so I finally laid it on and said, "Hey, you guys, I feel I produced." And they said, "Yes, you have, but just be patient. There's something happening. We can't tell you about it but we will deal with it."

I didn't know it at the time, but Ken Ritchie was retiring. When he retired, I got a phone call from Russ Cmolik wanting to know how much money I had. I said, "Russ, with the salary I'm getting, I don't have any money." But I was fortunate enough that I had borrowed $3,000, put it in the stock market, and sold it for $45,000. I gave that to the company as my down payment towards being a partner.[5]

The Brass Ring

Fortunately for Ritchie Bros., the new-equipment market in the United States wasn't faring any better than the one in Canada, opening the door for the Canadian auctioneer. In the early 1980s, Roger Rummel was hired from a Caterpillar dealer in Missoula, Montana, as one of the company's first United States sales representatives. Rummel recalled how Dave Ritchie convinced him to join Ritchie Bros.

"I had recently organized an auction with Ritchie Bros., and after the auction, Dave asked me to go to work for him," Rummel said.

But I was ready to go into the equipment business for myself. Still, Dave kept calling every week, saying, "You better reconsider." Then, on one December day when it was about 40 degrees below in Missoula, I got a call from Dave, and he said, "I'm sending you and your wife a plane ticket to Palm Springs to come down and take another look at us." At that point in time, Palm Springs sounded like a pretty good deal, so we flew down. I didn't know a lot about the company at the time, but when we got there, there was a big party going

on in the pool area and wine bottles in the hot tub. Then Dave and Dick Bartel put the full court press on, and I ended up going to work for them.[6]

The operation in the United States was ready to grow quickly. Already established throughout the western states, Ritchie Bros. moved east of the Mississippi in 1982 with a sale in Alabama.

Then in 1984 the company pulled off a coup in auctioneering. That year, Ritchie Bros. struck an agreement with Ring Power Corporation, a huge Caterpillar equipment dealer based outside Orlando, Florida. Ring Power had global sales and a national reputation among Cat dealers and had been selling equipment through auctions since the early 1970s, when it used them to "get rid of trade-ins," according to Randy Ringhaver, a principal at Ring Power.[7] At the time, Ring Power was selling most of its equipment through a U.S. auction company, but after four or five years, Ringhaver said his company became unhappy with what was happening at the auctions.

They would allow people to buy their equipment back, and we felt like that hurt our equipment because we were putting in primo-quality, late-model Caterpillar construction equipment and they were putting our equipment right next to somebody else's who was sitting there buying their equipment back. A lot of buyers became suspicious that we may be trying to

Above: Ritchie Bros.' unique ramp approach had helped revolutionize the auction industry. These bidders relax under the shade of a protective tent as they watch the machinery roll by.

Below: John and Doreen Ritchie, pictured in the early 1980s. By this time, John had already moved to South Africa and returned to Canada.

buy our equipment back, and we just didn't want to be associated with those auctions because we were putting a lot of business into them.[8]

Ring Power first approached Forke Brothers about auctioning its equipment, but the Nebraska company wouldn't bend on its commission, so when Ringhaver heard about a Ritchie Bros. sale in Nashville, he sent a delegation up to check it out.

"We were really impressed with the way they conducted the sale with the ramp instead of trying to move the people from piece to piece. They put the people in a stadium seating arrangement," Ringhaver remembered. Not only did the ramp make it easy for the bidders, but Ringhaver recognized it as a powerful selling tool for his company's equipment.

"Other people were putting in junk that wouldn't run, or the tracks would fall off and it wouldn't even make it across Ritchie's ramp," he said. "We felt like this was a way to differentiate our equipment. Plus Ritchie Bros.

CHAPTER SIX: COMING OF AGE   73

had a no-buyback rule that they were very adamant about."[9]

After watching the Nashville sale "go through the roof and becoming sort of infatuated with the process," Ring Power struck up an agreement that would establish Ritchie Bros. in the Florida market. Under this new agreement, Ring Power and Ritchie Bros. began to conduct a yearly auction just outside Orlando. The February Ring Power/Ritchie Bros. auctions quickly became a company tradition and kicked off each year's new auction season. As Cmolik remarked, "That Florida sale really became the crème de la crème."[10]

The Ring Power sales were valuable for even more reasons. In 1983, Ritchie Bros. recruited Bob Brawley, a salesman from Ring Power, and charged him with growing the United States operation as the newest Ritchie Bros. partner. "I was out in Los Angeles with Bob when Dave made the announcement to me that he had offered Bob Brawley a job," Ringhaver said. "I told Bob, 'Hey, this is a great opportunity for you.' "[11]

And it was. At the time Brawley joined, there were about five full-time employees generating gross sales of about $20 million a year in the United States. The company had an office in Portland, Oregon, and another small office in Montana and was active in several other states.

"Dave wanted us to pick some central location to start a U.S. head office, and I preferred Denver over someplace like Chicago," Brawley said. "When I arrived in Denver, we had no office and no operation. I got here in June and opened the first office. Dave

and Dick Bartel and Russ Cmolik had a package up in Canada from Ronny Miller and sent down a $2 million package for a sale in Denver. So we set up a sale date in August."[12]

That first week in Colorado, Brawley worked the telephone in a La Quinta Inn calling almost every contractor in the state of Colorado, looking for consignors. As more contractors added equipment, Brawley went out and rented a yard and trailer. The final sale produced about $5.5 million and was a great success. A second sale followed in October.

Almost immediately, Brawley hired Ken Asbury to run the Colorado business, which was growing quickly enough to warrant a permanent site. After an extensive search over several years, a 38-acre site was located. In 1985, Brighton, Colorado, became Ritchie Bros.' first permanent auction yard in the United States. By this time, the company had staged successful sales all across the United States, from Pennsylvania to California and from Texas to North Dakota.

These dump trucks are lined up in an auction yard before a sale. It was not uncommon to see prospective buyers climb up into cabs and start engines to evaluate a potential purchase.

111, now 112, 112, now I need 113, 113 one more time... get him, Rob! Your guy's out! 113, sir! Last call 113, thank you!

74   THE LEGEND OF RITCHIE BROS. AUCTIONEERS

The Advertising Function

As the number of permanent sites and sales grew, so did Ritchie Bros.' customer list. As a service organization, Ritchie Bros. depended for its success on the strength of its reputation and its potential buyers. Because of this, the company had always invested heavily in auction-day brochures and continued to seek high-profile advertising venues.

John Ivester, publisher of *The Last Bid*, clearly remembered the day he met Dave Ritchie and Dick Bartel. Ivester's magazine listed the sale prices and serial numbers of auctioned equipment. Designed as a reference source for both buyers and auction companies, *The Last Bid* became a frequent sight in the hands of participants at Ritchie Bros. sales.

"I was in Fairbanks, Alaska, in 1979 when Dave came up and introduced himself," Ivester said in a later interview. "We weren't covering Canada at the time, but we were getting ready to start. So Dave comes up and looks at our books and said he wanted to buy the cover ads. They bought every back-cover ad and other ads in our book for the next two decades."[13]

Helpful as they were, the ads were only one part of Ritchie Bros.' push for visibility. In the early 1980s, Bob Carswell was transferred from Calgary, Alberta, to the company headquarters in Richmond and given the job of streamlining and expanding Ritchie Bros.' advertising.

He made a number of administrative changes, including starting an inventory control system and bulk purchasing, but most importantly he overhauled the way Ritchie mailed out the auction brochures. These brochures were the calling cards of a Ritchie Bros. sale. They listed the items for sale and were an important part of the company's presentation to its customers.[14] By centralizing their production, Carswell was able to get more brochures out quicker—thus enlarging Ritchie's potential pool of customers. The advantages were readily apparent. In 1981, sales were around $100 million with 33 auctions. Only two years earlier, with the same number of auctions, sales had been $66.5 million.

The rise in sales mirrored a steady rise in Ritchie's publishing efforts. By 1985, sales had jumped to $203 million and the company had a list of 125,000 potential customers and was mailing out nearly 3 million color brochures every year to advertise its sales.

Big Auctioneering Comes of Age

This kind of major effort would have been unthinkable only 15 years before, but industrial auctioneering had matured since Ritchie's first big auction by the side of a mountain highway in Western Canada. How much of the change to credit to Ritchie Bros. would be hard to determine, but many people both inside and outside of the industry hasten to credit Ritchie's fundamentally different approach to auctioneering. The company's ramp was only the most visible sign—Ritchie Bros. had changed the way auction yards looked, the way consignors and owners sold equipment, and the way buyers viewed the company.

"The days of the backyard auctioneering are dying," proclaimed *Forbes* magazine in 1985. The article went on to report that auctions, excluding art, antiques, and agricultural products, were about an $85 billion business every year. Of that, real estate comprised $30 billion and the rest was heavy equipment, farm machinery, and aircraft.

One of the largest auctioneers, Ritchie Bros. Auctioneers International, specializing in heavy equipment, has more than doubled sales from 1980, and expects $175 million this year.

"Auctions are the purest form of capitalism," noted Brian Wannop, Ritchie's advertising manager.[15]

Rick Hullett, an equipment dealer in Montana, began attending Ritchie Bros. auctions in the early 1980s and would soon attend only Ritchie auctions. Like many other cus-

Dave Ritchie was the only Ritchie brother left in the company by the 1980s, and he remained deeply involved. Whenever possible, the founder jumped up on the platform and caught bids during the auctions.

Our salespeople are more than salespeople. They are consultants. They become confidants. In many instances, we're dealing with people that are selling through retirement, which isn't that difficult, but there are also sales where they're dealing with people who are suffering from illness or experiencing the death of a major shareholder or financial difficulties, marital breakups, partnership dissolutions. So the salesperson has to be able to deal with those issues in a compassionate and understanding way.[17]

The *Calgary Herald* agreed that Ritchie Bros. had changed the industry. In an article, the newspaper remarked that Ritchie Bros.' combination of business sense and personality had proved a winning combination.

Heavy industrial auctioneering has come of age as the most efficient way of disposing of surplus equipment only over the past 30 years.... Ritchie Bros.' success can be traced to an effective balance of personalities and talents. Dave Ritchie, the only brother still active in the business, is an idea man, dreamer and promoter. Dick Bartel, always cool, handles detail work and planning. Russ Cmolik provides the financial expertise.[18]

tomers, he also experienced firsthand the company's honesty after he had bought a piece of equipment that was listed as being 10 years newer than it actually was. "I called just to make sure their numbers were a little better," Hullett said. "I wasn't asking for money or anything. But about six weeks later, here comes a check for $3,000."[16]

This attitude, according to Ritchie Bros.' partners, developed because an auctioneer is different from a typical salesman on an equipment lot.

"Auctioning is different from retail sales," pointed out John Wild, who joined the company in 1981 after sporadic contact with Ritchie Bros. since the early 1960s.

To prosper throughout the 1980s was an achievement in itself. While Ritchie Bros.' gross sales were increasing on a yearly basis, the manufacturers of heavy equipment, such as Caterpillar, were sustaining heavy losses. Caterpillar reported a fourth quarter loss in 1982 of $204 million, while John Deere watched profits drop by 78 percent in the same quarter.

Ritchie enjoyed a strong market for used equipment and continued to seek out interesting and profitable spreads. In 1983, Ritchie Bros. was contracted to auction off the heavy equipment used in the construction of the Nandi and Lautake Regional Water Supply Dam in the South Pacific nation of Fiji. It was the first time Ritchie Bros. had been active in

Public
rb Auction
UNRESERVED

Dorval (Montréal), Québec

Mercredi,	Wednesday,
le 10 avril 1985	April 10, 1985
1:00 p.m. (heure locale)	1:00 p.m. (local time)

DOUGLAS DC3C

1976 PIPER SENECA II

RITCHIE BROS. Auctioneers
HEAD OFFICE: 9200 BRIDGEPORT ROAD, RICHMOND, B.C., CANADA V6X 1S1 TEL: (604) 273-7564 TELEX: 04-355580

the South Pacific and reflected Dave Ritchie's go-anywhere, sell-anywhere philosophy.

Two years later, Ritchie Bros. was contracted to stage a major liquidation of the Mannix family–held Loram International Ltd. in Calgary, Alberta. The sale was important for several reasons. First, the secretive Mannix family was powerful and famous in Canada's construction industry. Loram had been involved in projects including construction of Calgary's light rail transit line, the $13 billion Alsands project,

Above: This brochure was designed to advertise an aircraft auction. Because of Ritchie Bros.' success in heavy construction equipment, aircraft seemed like a perfect opportunity. The sales, however, were harder to administer and never caught on like Ritchie's traditional equipment auctions.

Right: Marty Pope joined Ritchie Bros. in 1980 and later became a partner. He was instrumental in helping the Edmonton operation expand rapidly.

and the Norman Wells pipeline enterprise. Second, Dave Ritchie was happy to get the deal for more private reasons: he had purchased the spread from Miller and Miller, the U.S. auctioneer and a Ritchie Bros. competitor.

"Some of my partners said I was crazy to buy it off Miller," Dave Ritchie remembered.

I had guys write letters to me, directors of the company, and say they didn't want to be any part of it and it was a very foolish move. But it was really the right thing to. If it hadn't happened, Miller would have come into our territory and gotten established, which I didn't really want. And we knew the deal real well. We'd been watching it very closely.[19]

As it turned out, it was a good move. The two-day Mannix auction was the largest ever in Calgary and attracted more than 1,400 bidders from across North America and Europe. "Buses have been leased to shuttle out-of-town buyers [to the auction]," reported the *Calgary Herald*. "Customs brokers will be on hand to process transportation permits and a bank will be represented to provide financing to buyers."[20]

Marty Pope, who started in 1980 in Vancouver and moved to Edmonton in 1984, remarked that the Mannix timing couldn't be better for the disposal of heavy construction and pipeline equipment. "The market is very strong right now," he said. "We've had calls on this from across North America and Europe."[21]

The sale ended up grossing nearly $13 million.

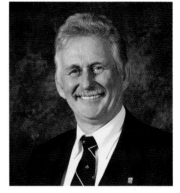

Taking to the Air

With such a strong market for used industrial equipment, it seemed like a good time to expand Ritchie Bros.' focus. The company that

to your man, Rob. Well done, bidder number 1472. The good bidders are certainly here today.

CHAPTER SIX: COMING OF AGE   77

had been so successful selling very expensive large machinery decided in 1983 to try selling another kind of very expensive equipment: private aircraft.

By 1985, Ritchie Bros. was ready with its first aviation-only auction. The first Canadian aviation sale was held in April 1985 in Montreal. This sale was soon followed by another strategic shift since, as Lawrence Sargenia, the firm's airplane specialist, pointed out, "There are only about 22,000 planes registered in Canada."

Ritchie Bros.' next airplane auction was arranged in the United States, at the Mesa Falcon Field in Phoenix, Arizona. The sale took place in February 1986 and was billed as the "first unreserved sale of planes in the United States." In standard Ritchie Bros. format, the airplanes were towed through an aircraft hanger, where all the bidders were seated. About 40 aircraft were sold for a total of $4 million.

Two auctions under its belt, Ritchie Bros. soon announced plans to hold several aviation auctions each year, including two in the Phoenix area. Airplanes were harder to source than industrial equipment, however, because, unlike construction machinery, there were no fleets of airplanes. Instead, Ritchie Bros. found itself with one-lot consignors.

"Each piece has a different owner, and you might have 30 or 40 airplanes in a sale and you'd have 30 or 40 owners," said Dick Bartel. "They did not understand the auction business. And at the time we went into it, the price of fuel was high and it was uneconomical to fly an airplane. We were selling them for what they were worth, but we didn't make the market."[22]

Ultimately, Ritchie Bros. decided to abandon aviation auctions.

Over the years, Ritchie Bros. often held sales and employee meetings in Palm Springs, California. Pictured is a group from an early 1980s sales meeting.

OK, now listen to me, gentlemen, we've got five tractors on the ramp, we're selling choice. Lots 672, 673, 674, 675, and 676.

78   THE LEGEND OF RITCHIE BROS. AUCTIONEERS

Corporate Changes: New Partners; Bartel Almost Retires

In 1986, still enjoying a strong used-equipment market, Ritchie Bros. invited three new partners into the company: Mark S. Clarke, James A. McKay, and Roger W. Rummel. This news, however, was soon offset by a surprise announcement from another partner. Dick Bartel, who had been with Ritchie Bros. since the company's very earliest days, announced he wanted to retire. He was 51 years old.

The April 29, 1986, newsletter announced the news, saying, "It is difficult to think of Ritchie Bros. Auctioneers without picturing that quiet, competent man handling the executive function of the company.... Dick starts a new phase of his life at the end of April when he retires to his apple orchard in Kelowna.... Russ Cmolik and Bob Carswell will be handling Dick's job."[23]

According to Don Chalmers, who joined the company in Edmonton in 1983 and became a partner in 1993, Bartel was an important foil for Dave Ritchie. "He was able to complement Dave by having a very valid opinion whenever Dave had a plan," Chalmers said. "Dick's contribution to the planning and the organization and the stability was great. He was involved in the valuation of each and every deal that Ritchie Bros. looked at."[24]

When asked what he would miss the most, Bartel said he would miss the people at Ritchie Bros. Naturally, plans were soon made for a gala send-off party, and the company began to prepare for Bartel's departure. Yet something strange happened at the party.

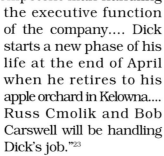

"He came up to me and he said, 'Dave, I don't know about this retirement,'" remembered Dave Ritchie. "I walked right over to the microphone and said, 'Dick just announced he's not retiring!'"[25]

According to Dave Ritchie, Bartel had always hoped to retire once he hit a certain level of financial comfort and, maybe even surprising himself, ended up with enough money to retire early and buy the apple orchard in Kelowna where he used to pick apples as a child. But during the party, surrounded by the people he had worked with for so long, Bartel realized that he would miss the business too much and changed his mind on the spot. The next day, as he had for nearly 30 previous years, Bartel reported for work.

Across the Pond

The addition of Mark Clarke to Ritchie Bros.' partnership foreshadowed even greater horizons for the company. Besides being a favorite among Ritchie Bros.' employees, Clarke would later head up the company's European operations, scouring the continent for buyers and promoting North American sales. Throughout the years, European bidders were a common sight at Ritchie Bros. auctions, and just about

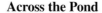

Above center: Dick Bartel joined Ritchie Bros. when the company was still headquartered in Kelowna and followed it to Vancouver and around the world. In 1986, Bartel—by then the number-two man in the operation—decided to retire but changed his mind at the last minute.

Above left: When Dick Bartel almost retired, Bob Carswell was in line to step up with Russ Cmolik and assume some of his duties. Pictured in 2000, Carswell was already a partner in the company in 1986.

Who'll give me fifty thousand, 50, 50, do it quickly... now 60, thank you!... now 70, 7... 70 thousand, 70, 70, 70, now 80, now 90,

CHAPTER SIX: COMING OF AGE 79

the time that Bartel reconsidered his retirement, the company began to consider launching European operations.

The first step was to choose a location for a Ritchie Bros. office. The ideal site needed easy access to good transportation networks and free-port status. After an extensive search, Ritchie Bros. announced it was opening an office in Rotterdam, in the Netherlands.

Ian Dawson, who helped Ritchie Bros. open the office and was fluent in several languages, explained in *Roundup* why Rotterdam was a natural choice: "Because it is neutral ground. If we were to establish the office in France, we would find it difficult to deal with those who speak English. The French are rather touchy about the use of English in their land. If we established ourselves in Great Britain, France and the French-speaking countries would ignore us. In Holland, we can approach everybody including the Middle East."[26]

In addition to the new location in Rotterdam, the company had 11 offices in Canada and 10 in the United States. There were permanent yards in Edmonton, Vancouver, Prince George, and the newly opened yard in Brighton, Colorado. In the previous 12 months, according to Ken Asbury, regional manager for the U.S. central region, the company "had sold more than $200 million."

That gave Ritchie Bros. the distinguished reputation of being the biggest and best auction house in the world. Ritchie Bros.' claim to success is its aggressiveness. We have offices where our competitors do not. We have more offices in North America and cover a larger geographical area. Our staff is larger. We get out and go after it. The philosophy Dave Ritchie laid out is based on Ritchie Bros.' reputation as its bond. You never want a dissatisfied customer. We go to great pains to make sure we never have one.[27]

Geographic reach was definitely an important part of Ritchie Bros.' success. The cost of intercontinental shipping was continuing to drop, and worldwide exchange rates and economies made it logical to "think globally" in the used-equipment business. Moreover, the kinds of big deals that Ritchie Bros. looked for were few and far between, scattered around the world. One such deal was coming together due to the short but intense 1982 war between Great Britain and Argentina for control of the Falkland Islands. That year, Argentina occupied the British-controlled islands and touched off a massive and ultimately futile battle for the islands about 300 miles off its coast.

When the war was finished, Great Britain embarked on a massive reconstruction effort that rebuilt the shattered airport, dock facilities, and other infrastructure in the Falklands. Years later, when the work was completed, Ritchie Bros. was called in to sell off the surplus equipment.

In 1987, Ritchie Bros. crossed the Atlantic with its first sale in England. The Liverpool event featured equipment used to rebuild the Falkland Islands after the war.

when the sale finally began, Ritchie Bros. had assembled hundreds of items, of which 125 had been brought north from the Falkland Islands. Over the two days of the sale, Ritchie Bros. brought in $17 million, selling a range of equipment that included trucks, forklifts, agricultural tractors, loader backhoes, and a wide variety of other tools. The sale generated auction prices that were 10 percent greater than expected, and the most expensive piece of equipment to be auctioned was a four-year-old Caterpillar 245 excavator that sold for more than $200,000.

Falkland War Auction: Part Two

In Europe, meanwhile, word had spread that Ritchie Bros. Auctioneers was planning to hold a huge sale of equipment from the Falkland Islands reconstruction. The sale was to take place in April 1987, and European port cities competed intensely for the Canadian auctioneer's first sale in their territory. It was an important moment for Ritchie Bros., especially considering the long-term prospects of auctioning in Europe. The company considered several sites, including Rotterdam, where an office was already open, as well as Liverpool, England.

Eventually, it was decided to hold the sale at Liverpool. "It has all the facilities we need, plus the added advantage of enabling us to land the equipment into the Freeport, where we could defer payment of the import value added tax and import duty," commented a Ritchie Bros. employee to a local newspaper reporter.[1]

There were other reasons to select England. The U.S. dollar was strong overseas, and Ritchie Bros. executives figured the U.K. market would be eager to purchase equipment used in the successful Falkland Islands war effort.

The majority of the equipment, about 1,000 individual pieces, was shipped from the Falkland Islands to Liverpool on three freighters, the *Martindyke*, the *Mercandian Universe*, and the *Provide*. Incidentally, the *Provide*, which carried more than 3,000 tons of vehicles and equipment, had acted as a floating hotel and landing pontoon at East Cove on the Falklands. The ship was also sold by Ritchie Bros. at the Liverpool sale, making it the first and only freighter ever sold by the company.

The two-day auction in Liverpool was a success, raising more than 8 million pounds sterling. "It was a real great sale," said Dave Ritchie.

After the sale, it was one of the funniest nights. We were going to take a bunch of customers for dinner. Historically, I always start out with maybe eight or ten guys, so I made a reservation at this fancy restaurant and they accepted it. Then, of course, the guys

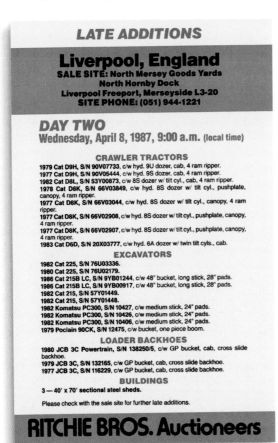

When word got out that Ritchie Bros. was planning a huge auction in England, additional consignors began adding equipment. This add-on was printed shortly before the successful sale.

CHAPTER SEVEN

GOING, GOING, GONE!

1987–1990

Ritchie Bros. has built a reputation that does away with the old auction image. The most highly skilled, knowledgeable team of auction experts in the industry make up the Ritchie Bros. team.... Ritchie Bros. is the leading industrial auctioneering company in North America.

—*Woodbridge Advertizer, 1987*

THE EFFORT TO REBUILD the Falkland Islands cost Great Britain hundreds of millions of dollars. By 1986, the Islands' airport had been reconstructed at a cost of more than $500 million, a new shipyard had been built, and new military facilities were completed. This work was performed by a joint venture, LMA, composed of John Laing Construction Ltd., Mowlem International Ltd., and Amey Roadstone Construction Ltd. The company brought a tremendous fleet of equipment to the islands; in all, more than 1,000 pieces of construction machinery were ferried across the oceans for the effort.

When the work was done, the material was purchased by Irish mogul Jim Mansfield of Mansfield's Truck and Machinery, who then entered into an agreement with Ritchie Bros. to auction off the equipment.

Obviously, the Falkland Islands were a less-than-ideal place to hold a heavy equipment auction, so Ritchie Bros.' management began sorting out the logistics of a truly global event. It was soon decided to split the equipment, sending part to the United States, where machinery made by North American manufacturers like John Deere and Caterpillar would be sold, and using the rest to introduce Ritchie Bros. into the European market.

In the United States, Ritchie Bros. elected to hold the huge auction in Atlanta, Georgia. The location was selected for a variety of reasons, and chief among them was Atlanta's pleasant climate on the chosen auction dates of October 15 and 16, 1986. Also, Atlanta's central location was perfect for this type of sale. About 800 miles south of New York, it could draw customers from the entire eastern seaboard of the United States, yet its being in the southern part of the United States meant bringing equipment by ocean from Argentina wouldn't be too difficult. Finally, Atlanta was a huge city with sophisticated transportation and equipment yards.

With the plan in place, other consignors added their equipment to the auction, and

---

As the machinery rolled by, workers used these signs to indicate which piece of equipment was the subject of the fast-paced bidding.

for choice, 125, 25, 25... last chance... 125... SOLD to your man, Eddie, for one hundred and twenty thousand dollars.

CHAPTER SEVEN: GOING, GOING, GONE! 83

start getting together and there's 10, then 15, and then there's 20. I kept calling the restaurant back to get more accommodations, and they finally say we can't take any more.

We end up going there, and by this time there's about ten carloads of people, and we all gradually work our way into the restaurant and start taking over the place. Around midnight, there was this guy Mansfield who had a daughter who was a professional Western singer from Ireland. She could sing Western music very well and we had a great time going. This fine restaurant had all of a sudden been taken over by a bunch of contractor-type guys.[2]

The party eventually moved over to a local pub, where it lasted until the very early hours—only to find the Ritchie Bros. team up early the next morning to catch a charter flight back to London, then a Concorde flight back to the United States for a sale in West Virginia, then back to England two days later to wrap up the after-sale details. Less than a week after that, Ritchie was in Sri Lanka, off the coast of India, where Ritchie Bros. acquired equipment used to build a canal for rice farmers. Over the weeks following the Liverpool sale, the company held additional sales in Ontario, Oklahoma, British Columbia, Saskatchewan, Arizona, Alberta, Virginia, New Mexico, Washington, Tennessee, Montana, Pennsylvania, and California.[3]

Ritchie Bros. was soon ready to open a second permanent office in Europe to complement Rotterdam. This time, the company selected Staffordshire, England.

Ritchie Bros., Texas Style

As the operation grew overseas, Ritchie Bros. continued to push into the lucrative United States market. Field offices were opened in Pennsylvania and Oklahoma. On February 26, 1987, following several years of success in Arizona, Ritchie Bros. celebrated the opening of a four-acre permanent auction site in Phoenix. Sales that year were

staged in some 30 states, grossing approximately $210 million.

While the company was definitely growing, there was still a horizon of opportunity in Texas. At the time, the company was holding three or four sales a year there and grossing between $15 million and $20 million. While this was a significant amount, it was only a fraction of the total auction market in Texas. For a variety of reasons, including local temperament and the presence of the oil and construction industries, Texas was a thriving auction market.

"I would say that the Texas market is probably the largest single state market anywhere in the world," said E. R. "Butch" Graham, an auctioneer who grew up in the auction business in Texas and Oklahoma. First a livestock and farm machinery auctioneer, Graham moved into industrial equipment auctioneering in 1980 and went to work for Ritchie Bros. in Texas in 1986.

Among the auction companies active in Texas was Miller and Miller, a family company run by Bill Miller, a car salesman who had started auctioneering in the 1950s after attending the Reisch American School of Auctioneering in Mason City, Iowa. In 1957, Miller held an oilfield truck sale in Shreveport, Louisiana, and over the next decade became very active in oilfield trucking-contract sales. In 1959, Miller and Miller competed successfully against Forke Brothers for a contract and staged its first $1 million auction. At the time, Forke Brothers was conducting nearly 90 percent of the equipment auctions in the United States, and Ritchie Bros. hadn't even been founded yet.

By the 1970s, Miller and Miller had become "the biggest thorn in Forke's side" and was conducting "almost all" of the equipment sales in Texas. At least some of this success was due to a lucrative contract with Halliburton, the Texas energy-field-services giant. Also, Miller benefited from winning a hotly contested contract in 1977 for the Trans-Alaska Pipeline. In one year, Miller and Miller's business doubled from around $65 million to over $120 million.

Throughout most of these early years, Ritchie Bros. wasn't a competitive threat. That began to change by the late 1970s, however, when Ritchie Bros. began to put pressure on the U.S. companies. "When Ritchie Bros. came into the United States, their competition forced us to go into permanent sites also," Miller said. "We established a permanent site in Fort Worth in 1979, about the time that they came along and really refined the auction business as far as the sale of heavy machinery is concerned."[4]

In 1987, Ritchie Bros. began a major push into the Texas auction market by opening a yard in Fort Worth. This shot of Ritchie's Texas yard was taken a decade later and suggests the magnitude of the company's largest U.S. operation.

By the time Ritchie Bros. partner Eddie Banser arrived in Texas in 1987, Miller and Miller was active at its Fort Worth site and grossing around $120 million per year. Ritchie Bros., by contrast, was grossing zero in the state.

"We had the office in a high-rise in downtown Fort Worth," Banser said. "One of the first things we did was to find a new place because that wasn't conducive to our business at all. We found a good piece of property on a major freeway, very close to the airport and in the middle of the metroplex. We leased it and put a building on it and began operating out of that yard."[5]

With the new location, new business began coming in, and the Ritchie staff began to grow. "We all worked hard," Graham said. "At that time, it was such a small, core group down here. But the thing that brought it together was

672 is gone, roll it off the ramp... and 675 and 676 are gone... mark those off in your books, gentlemen. Dennis,

CHAPTER SEVEN: GOING, GOING, GONE! 85

that Dave had the vision to come down here and hire people who had knowledge in this industry, had credibility in this industry, and had a clientele somewhat established."[6]

Before long, Ritchie Bros. had secured a steady source of business from highway contractors and general builders and had begun to secure equipment deals from Brown & Root, the engineering and construction giant. Before long, the Texas yard would grow into Ritchie Bros.' largest operation in the United States and eclipse Miller and Miller.

The Auction Company Next Door

The global used-equipment business, including the auction business, is a huge trade, measured in the tens of billions of dollars. No matter how big Ritchie Bros. got, the company could hardly hope to have more than a couple percent of the market.

"Auctions are only one way of disposing of equipment," said Dave Kruse, equipment sales manager for Peter Kiewet Sons Inc., a heavy construction company. "We also sell some of our own used equipment and go through other brokers. What we try to do with equipment sales is keep our fleet fresh, so if work is slow in one region, we will look at disposing of some equipment."[7]

One of the issues the company had to deal with was its position within the complex global marketplace for industrial equipment. On one hand, because Ritchie Bros. sold used equipment, it seemed to compete with every equipment dealer, rental agency, self-motivated contractor, and broker in the world. Yet there were some crucial differences

I have good news for you. I have two left and your man was runner-up, he was with us all the way, does he want one?

86   THE LEGEND OF RITCHIE BROS. AUCTIONEERS

between other outlets for used equipment and Ritchie Bros.

"In a way, we don't compete with anybody," Cmolik said.

If you look at equipment distributors, we don't really compete with them. We don't add value that they do. We don't add warranties, delivery, financing, trades, and any of that stuff. We're staying out of that. We just guarantee good title. A lot of them find us competitive, but the savvy ones are doing business with us.[8]

Randy Ringhaver was one of those used equipment dealers who saw it both ways when it came to dealing with Ritchie Bros. Ringhaver, who was instrumental in setting up the annual Ring Power/Ritchie Bros. auctions in Florida, remembered being a little surprised at the auction company's appetite for business.

"After a couple years, Ritchie Bros. was even becoming a little bit of a competitor to us at Ring Power," he said. "Ritchie was going out and buying spreads of equipment and offering people guarantees, things that the auction industry really had never done before. They started putting so many reps out all over the country that all of a sudden the deals that I used to get for our used-equipment business were going to auction."[9]

The issue of competition would probably never be resolved and would likely always remain friendly because of the huge potential in the used-equipment market. This gigantic potential was part of the reason Dave Ritchie had wanted to move his company beyond the Okanagan Valley, beyond Canada, and finally beyond North America. And, by the late 1980s, Ritchie Bros. was beginning to become a global company with offices in both North America and Europe, buyers from all over the world, and business prospects all around the globe.

This far-flung business was supported from Vancouver, where in 1987 Ritchie Bros.

expanded its headquarters by purchasing an adjacent building.

The advertising department had become the company's secret weapon. Over the years, Ritchie Bros. had built a preeminent mailing list for its auction brochures. This list included more than 100,000 potential buyers and was a gold mine of targeted marketing information. (More than four tons of promotional material was mailed out for the Liverpool auction alone.) Ritchie Bros.' advertising and marketing department also kept histories of the equipment that the company sold: the sale price generated, its condition, and its make and year. This private database provided a valuable resource for appraisals.

By 1987, with all of this marketing information centralized in Vancouver, Ritchie Bros. began to envision the day when all of its offices would connect to the main database. As computer technology, long-distance transmission of data, and remote video advanced, the company even began to imagine the day when it could broadcast auctions and take real-time bids from several sites at once.

Into the Jungles

Typically, breaking into a new market meant landing one huge contract. The Falkland Islands reconstruction project was a good example. Ritchie Bros. had used the high-profile event and source of equipment to break into Europe. In 1987, the company landed a second contract that introduced it to a new continent while providing material for a second European sale. This time, Ritchie Bros. had been awarded a contract to auction off equipment used in the construction of the Transgabonese Railroad in West Africa.

Opposite: Even as the company expanded overseas, it continued to build permanent facilities at its many auction yards. Customers appreciated these venues.

The money is one hundred and twenty thousand, sir. SOLD! Bidder number 1689. He takes which one? He takes the

88   THE LEGEND OF RITCHIE BROS. AUCTIONEERS

Prospective buyers have only to register before an event to bid on equipment. Finance companies and banks were also present at auctions to make it easier for buyers to finance their purchases.

The railroad had been built with petroleum industry support, as well as loans from France, West Germany, and international organizations. Work began on the railroad in 1974. Five years later, the first section was completed. Four years after that, the second section was opened, and by 1983, engineers and construction crews had succeeded in threading the rail line through the region's dense rain forest.

Ritchie Bros. first became involved with the project when the Gabonese ministry, through a French auction company, asked Ritchie Bros. to submit a tender on the equipment. This was easier said than done. When the work was finally finished, recalled Sylvain Touchette, a Ritchie Bros. partner who had worked in Montreal and Europe, it took weeks to figure out exactly what was available for sale. "I was in West Africa about a month," Touchette remembered, "to look at equipment. It was spread out on 750 kilometers of railroad through the jungle."[10]

Working in equatorial Africa came with its own set of challenges—and not all of them related to transportation and climate, remembered Dave Ritchie. As he told *Truck/Logger* magazine, "There in Gabon, just prior to my arrival, there was a missionary's head on a stick that the locals had decided they wanted for lunch."[11]

The decision was made to move the equipment out of the remote country and split it among auction sites, including one in Europe and one in the United States. This time, however, instead of going to Liverpool and Atlanta, the material was shipped by sea to Rotterdam and Charleston, South Carolina. The combined sales were a success: the auctions grossed more than $23 million.

With successful European sales behind it, Ritchie Bros. continued to look for business in the Old World. "It was an exciting time," remembered Touchette, who traveled extensively in Europe buying equipment. "Some in Europe knew what the auction business was, and some knew a little bit about Ritchie. But for a lot of them, it was a new kind of business and a new way to sell equipment."[12]

front one... lot 673. OK, I have one left. The price is 120. Who wants it at 120? Take it now or I'll open it up. First hand... SOLD!

CHAPTER SEVEN: GOING, GOING, GONE!   89

Only months after the West African sale, Ritchie Bros. staged a second big sale in Rotterdam, this time featuring iron from nearly every country in the European Common Market. Over 600 pieces of equipment were offered for sale. To address the language diversity of European countries, Ritchie Bros. had brochures published in five different languages: English, Dutch, French, German, and Spanish.

Following this sale, Dave Ritchie made a presentation at the French Construction and Equipment show in Paris. As a featured speaker, he traced the history of the heavy industrial auctioneering business and explained the different types of auctions. Like their counterparts in North America, Ritchie was convinced, all equipment buyers and sellers could benefit from auctions. At the same time, the audience was impressed to hear that Ritchie Bros. had grossed an average of $1 million in auction sales for just about every day of 1987.[13]

Auction in the Sun

Back in more familiar territory, Ritchie Bros. was experiencing continuing growth with its Florida sales. In 1988, after a two-day sale that brought in more than $20 million, Ritchie remarked, "Of all our auction sites, Orlando is considered the premier auction event by our bidders. The weather, the location and the quality of the equipment make it ideal for many of them to plan trips to the sunny and warm South in February every year."[14]

This record was the second highest gross sales amount for any Ritchie Bros. auction (behind only the 1987 sale in Orlando). Huge events like these were highly anticipated by equipment buyers and Ritchie Bros.' employees alike, sometimes for the spectacle as much as for the opportunity. At one memorable sale, the company had put together an elegant,

elaborate party for its customers, only to have an alligator wrestler show up at Dave Ritchie's invitation. "Dave had just met him somewhere and told him to come out and put on a show at this hotel," remembered Butch Graham. "You never know what'll happen."[15]

And the hotel probably didn't mind either. The Orlando auction sales were important sources of revenue for local business and brought out-of-town visitors. The *Orlando Business Journal*, in covering the Ritchie Bros. auction, wrote that the buyers live in a silent world "where a discreet nod or a slight finger movement spells several hundred thousand dollars at a time."[16]

Far away from the Sun Belt, Ritchie Bros. opened a new auction site at Bolton, near Toronto, in March 1988. Like other permanent facilities, this auction yard was designed to be as customer friendly as possible. "They do

---

The Ring Power/Ritchie Bros. sales in Orlando, Florida, became an annual event that kicked off the auction season.

Bidder number? Bidder number, please... number 915, thank you. Well done. They're going fast today!

90   THE LEGEND OF RITCHIE BROS. AUCTIONEERS

everything first-class," Kruse, a regular auction buyer, remarked. "I've seen them bring out heaters for inclement weather or buses for participants to warm up in if it gets too cold. They try to make it comfortable."[17] The new facility featured a canopy-covered, heated drive-through accommodating 1,000 participants. The site covered 18 acres.[18] At the grand opening in 1987, Ritchie Bros. auctioned a 988B wheel loader with low hours and a D7H Caterpillar high-drive tractor. Both were the first of their kind to be auctioned in Ontario.

Later in 1987, Ritchie Bros. staged a sale in Montreal that featured equipment that had been used in Pakistan. Like the European sales and the African business, this was an indication of how global the auction business was becoming. And in 1988, Ritchie Bros. moved into yet another region with the opening of an office in Singapore.

By then, the company had a staff of 150 permanent employees.

Focusing on Customer Service

In 1989, Ritchie Bros. had emerged as one of the largest industrial auctioneers in the world and a widely recognized pioneer of modern industrial equipment auctioneering. Despite its size, the company maintained its intense customer loyalty, including the regular fishing trips up to Stuart Island and the preauction party and cocktail hour.

The Ritchie Bros. executive staff posed on a piece of "Big Iron" in the late 1980s. Dave Ritchie is at the top, standing near the cab.

CHAPTER SEVEN: GOING, GOING, GONE! 91

At the same time, the company's business services had evolved. Besides performing title searches to support its guarantee of clear title on all equipment it sold and offering early access to the equipment, Ritchie Bros. made available the names of consignors and encouraged the prospective buyers to do as much background checking on equipment as was possible. For consignors, the company provided a variety of auction locations, advice about and management of equipment refurbishing, extensive marketing programs, assistance with creditor issues, coordination of all dealings with prospective buyers, and the collection and disbursement of proceeds—a turnkey service for equipment owners that treated every customer equally.

Dave Husby, owner of Husby Forest Products in Maple Ridge, British Columbia, first bought a pickup truck at a Ritchie auction in 1970. By 1989, he was generating about $1 million of business a year with the company but said, "I was treated the same when I bought one old pickup truck as when I'm doing $1 million a year. Their customers are all treated the same, and they're all treated well."[19]

By the late 1980s, Ritchie Bros. was ready to offer an additional customer service by capitalizing on the rapid pace of technological innovation. In 1989, the company posted a first in its industry with a "live video" auction. Interestingly, this achievement was the product of a scheduling conflict. Ritchie Bros. had an auction at Nisku on the same late October day as the Edmonton AgriCom forestry show. Fearing that many of its customers would attend the show and hearing that the show expected 20,000 visitors, Ritchie Bros. arranged to "show what we were doing" at the forestry conference.[20]

In 1988, Ritchie Bros. continued its global push by opening an office in Singapore. Pictured touring the Hitachi factory are, left to right, Gil Hosier, Russ Cmolik, Dave Ritchie, and the representative from Hitachi.

Video cameras were set up in the auction yard, and the action was broadcast via satellite to a giant screen in the AgriCom, where interested bidders could participate in the sale by bidding live.[21]

With the steady increase in both the numbers of auctions being held by Ritchie Bros. and the volume of Big Iron inventory at each, Ritchie Bros.' sales were climbing. Between 1979 and 1989, the number of auctions nearly doubled, from 33 per year to 63 per year. Gross sales had multiplied more than sixfold, from $66 million in 1979 to $406.2 million in 1989. A great contributor to the growth of the Canadian Prairie Region during this time period was Glen Wyatt, a partner from 1981 until 1989 in Nisku, Alberta.

Ritchie Bros. was awarded the contract to auction the equipment used in the *Exxon Valdez* cleanup effort. Some of it was shipped to Tacoma, Washington, where crowds of buyers drove up the prices.

CHAPTER EIGHT

THE RIGHT RUNNING SHOES

1990–1997

I think I'm probably the luckiest guy on earth to have been part of an organization like this.

—Dick Bartel, 1999

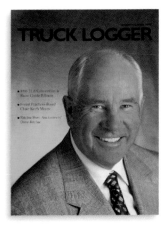

THE MARKET FOR USED construction and transportation equipment began to shift in the 1990s. When Ritchie Bros. first started auctioning in the early 1960s, equipment fleets were generally viewed as an indication of success for contractors. The larger the fleet, the more successful the contractor. In the 1990s, however, this was to change. Contractors, instead of building up massive fleets that might sit idle for a portion of the year, began to view their equipment as a more liquid asset. Equipment might be bought for a certain job to meet specific needs and then sold immediately afterward, or it might be leased.

"It used to be that you would ask a contractor how he was doing and he would tell you how many trucks he had," reported the *Engineering News-Record.* "Today, pride of ownership is on the wane and equipment is a business entity more than ever."[1]

Because of this, many large contractors began to pare down their fleets. The trend was ideal for Ritchie Bros., which specialized in quickly converting unutilized equipment into cash. The company kicked off the decade with a colossal sale on May 15 in Orlando. With gross sales of $27 million, it was the largest one-day sale in the history of industrial equipment auctioneering.

"We sell it for fair market value," said Ritchie Bros. partner Ed Banser. "But the real advantage here is that it may take six months to a year to sell a truck parked and idle. We do it in less than a minute and that guy gets his check in 21 days. It's immediate and it's clean."[2]

The used-equipment market was also helped by the manufacturers themselves, who began to pay more attention to the after-market as more contractors turned to used machines. In the 1990s, John Deere began offering incentives on its used machines, including the transfer of powertrain warranties and free updating of safety improvements. Other manufacturers, including Caterpillar, took similar steps.

In its December/January 1996 issue, *Truck Logger* magazine featured an extensive interview with Dave Ritchie. By then, his company had become the most successful and largest industrial auction house in the world.

Ritchie Bros. was in an excellent position to capitalize on these emerging trends and had no intention of sitting idly by as the industry developed. Instead, it planned to lead the equipment auction business with a variety of strategies.

First, the company planned on holding more auctions with the aid of ever-greater leading-edge technologies. Fresh from auctioning off equipment used in a pipeline project across Russia, Dave Ritchie told *Equipment World* magazine:

Technology will do even more to bring equipment buyers together. I hope to see high definition television develop so that we could conduct auctions in Vancouver and have customers from all over the world bid. They'd be able to see the equipment and we'd be able to see them bid. I envision one day that you'll see a bank of TV cameras at these auctions. This is only a premonition of things to come.[3]

Second, with gross auction sales of about $450 million in 1990, Dave Ritchie envisioned a whole world of opportunity. Just as Ritchie Bros. had expanded across North America in the 1980s, it planned to go around the world in the 1990s. Randy Wall, who joined Ritchie Bros. in 1988, helped plan for the major global expansion. "The business was coming," Wall remembered, "and there were these big projects that resulted in large packages of equipment that could be used to start an auction. Those days were extremely exciting."[4]

At the time, Ritchie Bros. had established offices in Europe, where the regular sales at Rotterdam were still growing, and Singapore. The overseas business was successful, but nowhere near what Ritchie Bros. hoped to someday record. As far as the Ritchie Bros. crew saw it, there were ripe auction grounds in Australia, Southeast Asia, the Middle East, eastern Europe, parts of Africa, and South America.

Ritchie Bros. would move on as many fronts at the same time as it could and announced in 1990 that it was time "to enter the whole Southeast Asia market very actively within the very near future through our Singapore office. The Southeast Asia market represents about 33 percent of all the iron in the world today. The growth factor there is incredible. We just need a faster pair of running shoes to keep up with it all."[5]

The *Exxon Valdez* Sale

Yet first there were other deals waiting to happen closer to home: Ritchie Bros. soon found itself playing a part in a global drama. One March night in 1989, at 12:04 A.M., far north in the oil-port town of Valdez, Alaska, the massive *Exxon Valdez* ran aground on Bligh Reef and began to pour oil into the pristine waters of Prince William Sound. The effort to stop the flow of oil or contain the spill was hampered by strong winds and waves, and by the time the disaster was contained, 10.1 million gallons of crude oil had poured into the sound and beyond the reach of containment. Sadly, the accident polluted thousands of miles of convoluted and untouched shoreline, eventually traveling as far south as the end of the Alaskan peninsula.

The reaction to the world's greatest oil spill was intense. Environmental groups, who had feared exactly such a calamity, petitioned the government for retribution. Exxon, meanwhile, launched a cleanup that would eventually cost more than $1 billion. For two summers after the spill, armies of specialists, volunteers, and employees scoured the waters and shoreline of the fjord in an attempt to rescue local birds, sea otters, seals, and other wildlife.

When the cleanup effort was finally over, the Ritchie Bros. team went after the equipment. Dave Ritchie shuttled between Exxon's Houston headquarters and Anchorage, accompanied by fellow Ritchie Bros. employees, as he tried to secure a contract from Exxon. One was finally signed, and Ritchie Bros. found itself with a bewildering assortment of supplies and material for sale. In preparation for the auction, 16 office workers and more than 50 yard personnel were hired to supplement the Ritchie crew. The company organized a four-day sale in Anchorage, Alaska, in October 1990, when to more than 8,000 registered bidders it auctioned off 9,768 lots of equipment "grouped to appeal to individuals, contractors, outfitters, hotels, and used equipment dealers," said Rob Mackay, a Ritchie Bros. vice president.

The diversity of the items for sale was staggering. The sale included danger signs, wheelbarrows, portable bathrooms, water coolers, life rafts, inflatable boats, anchors, buoys, fish net, cork, bottles of shampoo, fire extinguishers, winches, immersion suits, passenger buses, cars, vans, trucks, and even medical supplies.

"Everything about the *Exxon Valdez* oil spill was expensive, but last week it produced a few bargains," reported *Time* magazine. "At an auction in Anchorage to sell off surplus equipment ... buyers bid on acres of items ranging from animal shampoo to mobile homes to microwave ovens."[6]

The gross sales were in excess of $14 million, and this respectable amount didn't even reflect the entire inventory. Some of the equipment and material intended for use in Alaska had remained in Tacoma, Washington, and

Ritchie Bros. shipped still more from Alaska to Tacoma. That fall, the second *Exxon Valdez* sale grossed $6 million.

This page: There was an amazing diversity of items up for sale at the *Exxon Valdez* event. Buyers bid on inflatable boats, gear, outboard motors, and thousands of other items not normally seen in Ritchie sales.

"It turned out that, in fact, we probably should have left it all in Alaska," Bartel later said. "We didn't think we'd get enough people up there, but they'd created so much interest that it would have sold just as well there."[7]

At the close of 1990, Ritchie Bros. had 34 permanent offices throughout the world and was conducting 70 auctions per year. It had taken the company 21 years to generate its first billion dollars in total sales and a mere three years to generate its second billion dollars.

Dick Bartel Retires; A Building Spree

In 1991, five years after his abortive attempt to retire to an apple orchard in the Okanagan, Dick Bartel again announced he was planning to retire. This time, at the age of 56, the longtime company leader was true

This permanent yard in Tampa, Florida, was opened as part of a building spree in the early 1990s. Much of the new development took place in the United States.

to his word. In April 1991, Dick Bartel left Ritchie Bros. to divide his time between the orchard in Kelowna and his home in Phoenix, Arizona. Bartel, like all of the long-time employees and partners, had been instrumental in building Ritchie Bros. and would be much missed throughout the company.

Bartel's retirement coincided with the beginning of a building spree that lasted three years. A Ritchie Bros. yard, with its covered auction theater, permanent ramp, and other amenities, was vastly preferable to leased sites. Between 1991 and 1994, land was purchased or yards were opened in Tampa, Florida; Lakeville, Minnesota; Fort Worth, Texas; Brighton, Colorado; and Olympia, Washington. At the same time, new offices were opened in Oakland, California; Tampa, Florida; Albuquerque, New Mexico; Odessa, Texas; and Vanersborg, Sweden.

to buyer 278. A good eye and a good buy. Thank you, sir.

98   THE LEGEND OF RITCHIE BROS. AUCTIONEERS

This building spree met the demand generated by an increasingly strong used-equipment market. "Demand for machines has sparked a renaissance in equipment resale during the past five years, and the average used machine sale price has climbed 12 percent since 1989," reported *Construction Equipment* magazine. "Auctioneers are setting up enormous sales centers with pavilions to shelter buyers and offer all the necessary amenities to make the buying process easy."[8]

By 1994, the *Gazette* in Montreal reported that Ritchie Bros. had generated around $650 million in sales.[9]

First Video Auctions

The new facilities were good for both customers and Ritchie Bros., which was beginning to experiment with new technology in its tried-and-true auction format. In 1993, Ritchie Bros. hosted the industry's second live video auction. This event was held in conjunction with ConExpo '93, an equipment and industry show in Las Vegas. A giant projection screen at ConExpo was set up to show the ConExpo attendees a sale live and in progress at the Olympia yard in Washington.[10]

The broadcast of both audio and video was carried by satellite one way from the Olympia auction site to ConExpo. It was one way only, meaning Las Vegas bidders could see the auction and bid on it but the crowd in Olympia could not see the ConExpo bidders. This first attempt met with some success. Successful ConExpo bidders bought machines, and Ritchie Bros. began to incorporate broadcast capabilities in all its auction facilities under construction or being planned.

Two years later, in 1995, the company took another step toward remote auction technology by using a high-speed fiber-optic video and audio feed to connect an auction in Fort Worth, Texas, with delegates attending the 76th Annual Associated General Contractors of America convention in San Diego.

The Auction Heard Round the World

While the experimenting with technology was done slowly and cautiously, beginning in 1993 Ritchie Bros. aggressively expanded overseas. The company sought opportunities everywhere and pursued them, calling on local contractors all over the world and soliciting new business. Ritchie Bros. had done this before, buying equipment from Sri Lanka (where Dave Ritchie got to ride elephants) and shipping it to San Diego, or shipping equipment from Gabon, Africa, to Rotterdam (the freight bill alone was more than $1 million). But over the next years, Ritchie Bros. would shift its strategy: new spreads would be used to open up new markets.

Like all Ritchie Bros. expansions, it was a group effort but handled by surprisingly few people. Dave Ritchie, of course, was instrumental in tracking down big sales, as was Russ Cmolik. Mark Clarke traveled extensively throughout Europe, while Rob Mackay patrolled the Asia-Pacific region. At any given time, Ritchie Bros. had employees bidding on and auctioning equipment in five or six countries as the company spread its arms in an exciting flurry of global plane rides, new sites and cultures, and, as always, the pursuit of high-quality equipment and new experiences.

"We got to experience some phenomenal scenery and local cultures," reminisced Rob Mackay of these years. "You get to eat all kinds of things that you better not ask what it is. Some guys don't take to it well, but other guys don't bat an eye and just have at it, take it all in stride, and it's an exciting time for them."[11]

In 1994, Ritchie Bros. officially introduced itself to Mexico with a big sale. The deal was put together by Russ Cmolik, who negotiated a contract with an Italian company that had just built a hydroelectric dam in Zimapan, Mexico. On December 17, 1994, the papers were finally signed, and Ritchie Bros. quickly put together its first auction in the country.

Two days after the deal was signed, however, the Mexican peso was halved in value and interest rates doubled overnight. "We lost

Here's the star of the show. You've been eyeing this crane all day, now we're going to sell it. Lot 774, gentlemen. Give me

CHAPTER EIGHT: THE RIGHT RUNNING SHOES   99

a ton on the auction," said Cmolik. "But we performed every obligation pursuant to the contract and then some. We went above and beyond the call of duty."[12]

In keeping with a Ritchie Bros. tradition that the "guy who does the most difficult deal during the year" has to attend the yearly partners' meeting wearing a hat from the unlucky sale, Cmolik sat through the 1994 partners' gathering wearing a sombrero.

Almost at the same time but all the way around the world, Cmolik and Mark Clarke were busy pursuing another deal. After the Gulf War between Iraq and coalition forces led by the United States, a massive rebuilding project was initiated in Kuwait, where Iraqi forces had destroyed buildings and uncapped oil wells throughout the country.

"That was a tremendously interesting job," Cmolik remembered of the 1993 negotiations.

We went to Kuwait and we trudged all through the areas where the fires were. Mark and I had to drive all the way from Kuwait City up through to Basra on the Kuwaiti highway. It was shelled all through there, and we were maneuvering through the shell holes on the road.

But there was a lot of machinery. First they had to put the fires out, and then they had to try to corral the oil. We had a crew all through that area and did a deal with the Kuwait Oil Company and bought all that equipment that was used to fight fires and to do construction and cleanup. We brought it out and sold it in Houston, England, and Rotterdam.[13]

The equipment was all fairly new, low-hour equipment, but it had been modified for use in the extreme desert conditions. "You could see where they had tacked on the heat shields, then cut them off with a torch," Cmolik said. "There were nubs on some of it."[14]

Seeing even more opportunity in the oil- and construction-rich region, Clarke and Cmolik continued to buy used equipment and began hoping to establish an auction ground. In 1996, Ritchie Bros. pursued a contract to auction off the equipment in the United Arab Emirate of Ash Sharjah, but negotiations stalled at the last minute.

"We had all this equipment parked on the beach in Kuwait and we just let it sit there," Cmolik said. "In the end it took us a year to finalize the venue for that auction, and we eventually moved the equipment to Dubai. We lost money on the sale. Pioneering has its challenges!"[15]

The Subic Experiment

Maybe the most important expansions, however, took place in the Far East. With its "faster pair of running shoes" on, Ritchie Bros. launched an aggressive campaign to move throughout Asia and the Pacific Rim. The company already had a toehold in Australia, where it had staged a successful sale in 1990 on behalf of a Caterpillar deal.

But what Ritchie Bros. really wanted was a regional hub where buyers from all over the Asia-Pacific region could travel for buying and selling. In 1994, a package of equipment became available in the port city of Subic Bay, the Philippines. Instead of moving it out, Dave Ritchie decided to open up a new region.

"Ritchie Bros. needed a central site in Asia to conduct its auctions of tractors, front-end loaders, graders, etc.," reported the *Financial Post* in Toronto.

It wanted lots of space, access to water-front facilities, and preferably a site with free-port status so it wouldn't have to pay duties or tariffs on equipment being shipped in or out. Subic met all these conditions.

The company brings in used equipment from Korea, Dubai or Indonesia, for example, and buyers come to the Subic site to buy it at auction. Ritchie Bros. then helps the buyers arrange shipping to Australia, Malaysia, Singapore or elsewhere.[16]

Until 1992, most of the Subic Bay free port had been a U.S. military base. From there, the

United States military had staged operations in both the Vietnam War and Operation Desert Storm. That year, however, the U.S. military shut down operations and the Philippine government began looking for new tenants. For Ritchie Bros., Subic Bay seemed to be a good potential location. It was a major port with some transoceanic shipping, it was a duty-free zone, and the surrounding community was populated by a well-trained and educated workforce who used to work at the military base.

But Subic Bay also had its share of built-in challenges. Rob Mackay and Peter Blake, an accountant who joined Ritchie Bros. in 1991, spearheaded the project to get established in the Philippines and quickly discovered that the country sometimes seemed mired in red tape and bureaucracy, not to mention the cultural differences within the island nation.

"In our first auction sale, a fair bit of equipment had come up from Manila from this American contractor," Mackay said.

One of the trucking companies, a local Filipino company, was hauling the stuff up from Manila, and as he approached Subic Bay, he swung his truck out wide to get into the entrance gate. But right beside the highway, as they do in the Philippines, there was a burial ground. He knocked over a headstone, which just about caused an international incident. We ended up buying the family a new headstone, and the truck was under seizure for a couple days.[17]

Worse yet, the site was the victim of local politics and wasn't on the international shipping lanes. Consequently, Ritchie Bros. found

In the mid-1990s, Ritchie Bros. opened up an auction yard in Subic Bay, the Philippines. The site was originally designed to act as a hub for the whole Pacific region, but plans changed, and Ritchie Bros. shifted its focus to Singapore.

300, now 25, 25, three twenty-five... no, Jim, you're out, I recognized Larry at 300, I need three-twenty-five from your man,

CHAPTER EIGHT: THE RIGHT RUNNING SHOES   101

that it could maintain a business in Subic Bay, but most of the buyers at the sale were actually from the Philippines—it wasn't the regional hub they had hoped for.

"It was an interesting time," Blake said.

It was a useful market for a time, but we were looking for more of a hub to attract all of Asia. Plus, guys that were coming in had trouble getting everything shipped in and out of Subic Bay. So we thought, "What are we doing in Subic? Everything we're selling here is staying in the Philippines because we're not attracting that international audience."[18]

Instead of fighting an uphill battle, Ritchie Bros. shifted its strategy and began focusing on Singapore, which was ideally located and, because of the meltdown in Asian economies, welcomed the new business. Or, as Mackay later put it, "Singapore was a cake walk compared to the Philippines."[19] It took about a year to locate land and secure a long-term lease.

Also during that period, Ritchie Bros. continued to push into Australia. In 1995, the company announced it was opening an office in Brisbane, Australia. The first sale from that office took place in July and generated gross auction sales of about $14 million (AUD). The company established a permanent presence in Australia in 1997. "Ritchie Bros. Auctioneers' branch in Brisbane has not let the grass grow under its feet since running a large auction on March 11, 1997, in Brisbane," according to the *Mining Journal.* "It has next secured the rights to auction the entire fleet of mining equipment from the Ebenezer coal mine."[20]

The Island That Wasn't

As Australia expanded, Asia itself soon added a high-profile sale to the company's history of big events. The story of this sale began years before, when the regional airport serving Hong Kong became crowded to capacity and city leaders decided to build another. In the coastal city, however, land was scarce and at

Tall order to spruce up giant trucks

Big brush-up ... cleaning a massive dump truck is a daunting task at the best of times – so sprucing up 37 of them in time for today's auction is an extremely tall order. The trucks have travelled the equivalent of more than four times around the world in the three years they have hauled rock and sand around the new airport site at Chek Lap Kok. They and several huge excavators capable of ripping out more than 200 tonnes in a single bucket-load are no longer required. More than 100 potential buyers from around the world are likely to roll up for the auction which is expected to raise about $85 million, according to Canadian auction company Ritchie Bros. This is a fraction of the $1 billion paid for the equipment when work began in 1992. "It is the first time Hong Kong has seen anything like it," said Ritchie manager Andrew Hornsby.
– KEITH WALLIS

In 1996, Ritchie Bros. sold off equipment used to build the Chek Lap Kok Island Airport in Hong Kong. The ambitious airport project built an entire island using huge earth-moving equipment.

a premium, so engineers looked to the next closest thing: the sea. Plans were set to construct the single largest project ever made by humans, a giant airport on a man-made island just off the coast. The resulting Chek Lap Kok Island Airport was an engineering masterpiece.

In order to build the airport platform, Japan-based Yamazaki Construction Company had flattened Chek Lap Kok Island and a neigh-

325, 25, 25, now 350, 350, 350, three hundred and fifty thousand dollars, now 375, 75, 75, I have 350, need 75, 75, 75, try

102   THE LEGEND OF RITCHIE BROS. AUCTIONEERS

boring island for supplies of rock. This rock had then been used to build an island upon which the airport itself was constructed. All told, about 80 percent of the world's dredging capacity was used to move 45 million cubic meters of material, much of it granite.

Rob Mackay had a contact within Yamazaki and went after the equipment. All told, there was a huge fleet of equipment ready for auction, including about ten Caterpillar 785 dump trucks, 30 trucks, eight Cat dozers, and three massive electric face-shovels capable of ripping out 200 tons of rock in one bucket load.

"When Mr. Yamazaki started winding down on the leveling of the island, we started calling on them and contacting them," Mackay said. "They put out a list of equipment that they were selling and started to market it on a piecemeal basis."[21]

Watching Yamazaki sell his own equipment wasn't what Ritchie Bros. wanted to do, but the company had no choice but to watch from the sidelines. Eventually, Yamazaki found a buyer in Australia who was willing to pay around $400,000 each for the newest 785 rock trucks. While this wasn't a bad return, Yamazaki was frustrated with the length of time and the amount of effort it took to sell the trucks. Finally, he turned to Ritchie Bros. and set up a deal to sell everything through auction.

The January 1996 auction sale was complicated, however, by the Hong Kong Airport Authority, which wouldn't allow a sale on Chek Lap Kok itself. Instead, Ritchie Bros. had to ferry prospective buyers to and from the island so they could inspect the equipment, but hold the actual sale in a hotel ballroom. All told, the $10 million sale took about an hour and twenty minutes. During the auction, trucks identical to the ones that Yamazaki had sold for around $400,000 fetched $575,000 each—another testament to the power of an auction.

Only months later, Ritchie Bros. was again called upon to sell equipment used in a huge project, this time a bridge in England. The Second Severn Crossing Bridge, constructed by

Laing-GTM, was designed to cross the Severn River in England. The three-mile-long bridge took four years to complete and was one of Europe's longest marine civil-engineering projects. Ritchie arranged to sell the equipment in June 1996 near Bristol. Besides an array of trucks, boats, and vehicles, the auction bill included a huge launching gantry that had been used to place sections of bridge and a powerful water jet.

Bridge projects were nothing new to the company. Three years before, Rob Mackay had put together a deal to sell equipment used to build the Stoerbelt Bridge linking the city of Copenhagen, which sits on an island, to the Danish mainland. While working on the deal, Mackay moved his whole family to Denmark for the summer, where they lived in a small Danish-speaking town in the countryside.

With Stoerbelt successfully completed, Ritchie Bros. next secured a contract to sell

Bridge gear goes under hammer as auctioneers get heavy

SHIP AHOY: One of the lots at today's auction of Second Severn Crossing equipment

BIGGEST SALE OF CENTURY!

THE sale of the century was under way today as machinery used to build the giant Second Severn Crossing went under the hammer.

Buyers flocked to the auction at Severn Beach, which was expected to see several million pounds changing hands.

Giant concrete mixers, cranes, bulldozers, lorries, heavy plant - and even a fleet of small boats - were up for grabs.

Canadian auctioneers Ritchie Brothers brought their trans-Atlantic sales style to the event.

They were brought in by bridge builders Laing-GTM to sell off millions of pounds of gear.

The team of auctioneers kept up a rapid-fire patter as they began selling more than 500 lots.

The auctioneers kept up a breathless banter selling up to 100 lots an hour at anything from a few pounds to tens of thousands.

■ Turn to Page 2

HUGE INTEREST: Crowds flock to the sale site near Severn Beach

360... 360, thank you, now 370, 370, 370, three hundred and seventy thousand dollars... Anyone at 370? 370 YES! Now 380,

CHAPTER EIGHT: THE RIGHT RUNNING SHOES 103

Bridge-building leftovers on block

An auctioneer in Borden, P.E.I., calls for bids yesterday on surplus odds and ends used in co[...] of the Confederation Bridge. Bargain hunters from far and wide have converged to pick thro[...] overs ranging from wrenches to trucks. The two-day auction is expected to collect some $4 m[...]

Both pages: Ritchie Bros. continued to hold big-event sales. Shortly after the Hong Kong sale, the company sold equipment used in the construction of the Second Severn Crossing Bridge in England, facing page (Picture courtesy *Bristol Evening Post & Press*), then followed that with the sale of material used in the Prince Edward Island bridge project in Canada, above.

equipment used to build the Confederation Bridge, which linked Prince Edward Island to the Canadian mainland. The bridge had taken almost 6,000 workers three years to build, and it spanned almost 13 kilometers between New Brunswick and Prince Edward Island. The sale took place in the summer of 1997.

"I'm going to guess that there's probably enough extension cord to go around the world," Terry Christopher of Ritchie Bros. told the *Toronto Star*.[22]

The Advent of the Internet

The video auctions had met with some success, but another industry revolution was coming. By 1996, the Internet was promising to overhaul the way business was conducted in North America and held the promise of transforming commerce the world over. Although the Internet could transmit sound and video, early video streaming technology had built-in lag times which made it too slow to match the rapid pace of a Ritchie Bros. auction.

Ritchie Bros. was enthusiastic about the possibilities of the Internet and quick to launch one of the first auction Web sites. Clay Tippett helped the company develop its first Web site. "I asked Dave if he ever heard of the Internet, and he said he had. And I asked him if there was any reason why we wouldn't want to have all of our equipment on-line. He said he thought it was a good idea."[23]

now 390, 390, 90, 90, 90, one more time, sir? At three hundred and ninety thousand... 390, 90, 90, 90, and I have... FOUR HUNDRED,

104   THE LEGEND OF RITCHIE BROS. AUCTIONEERS

The ConExpo/Conagg of March 1996 in Las Vegas was used as the event to launch the new Web site, rbauction.com.

It featured a searchable database, which was updated every night, containing details of all the items to be sold in the upcoming auctions as well as an auction calendar with links to details about the individual auction events.

"Once a package of equipment is signed to one of our auctions, there will be instant information available to interested buyers of trucks and construction equipment," said Ken Dunn, manager of information systems for Ritchie Bros.[24]

At the unveiling, Ritchie Bros. staff provided "Live on the Internet" demonstrations.

"Ritchie Bros. is more than familiar with the old ways of doing things," commented *Business Watch* magazine. "Dave Ritchie has also explored different ways to do business in today's high-tech world. The company's Web site has about 300 hits per day.... It's helped to increase volume."

Reorganizing

Throughout all this time, Ritchie Bros. had operated as a partnership. In 1997, however, Ritchie Bros. reorganized under a single Canadian corporate parent called Ritchie Bros. Auctioneers Incorporated.

At the time of the reorganization, the company had 313 full-time employees, about 1,000 part-timers, and seven auctioneers under exclusive contract.

To the Middle East

While the company used its office in Singapore to expand through the Asia-Pacific region (sales were held in New Zealand and Tokyo in 1997), Ritchie Bros. still hadn't met with success in its search for a hub office in the Middle East. The negotiations were ongoing, however, and in late 1997 finally bore fruit. Ritchie Bros. had secured access to a site in the United Arab Emirates in Dubai. Besides

being friendly to Western business interests, the country was perfect because it "is ideally located as it has many shipping lines passing through and the rates are more reasonable. This is very important to us as the machinery is shipped to our auction sites by the original owners at their own cost," said Glen Day, Middle East sales manager for Ritchie Bros.[25]

The first Ritchie Bros. sale was held in the Jebel Ali Free Zone in Dubai on October 14–15, 1997. Unlike many sales, which are organized in a matter of months, this sale took "a year to

2

RITCHIE BROS. Auctioneers

دبي ، الامارات العربية المتحدة

Dubai
United Arab Emirates

الثلاثاء ١٤ اكتوبر و الاربعاء ١٥ اكتوبر ١٩٩٧

Tuesday, October 14, 1997
& Wednesday, October 15, 1997

وقت البدء ٩ صباحاً
9:00 a.m.

موقع البيع : ص . ب . ١٦٨٩٧
المنطقة الحرة لجبل علي
دبي ، الامارات العربية المتحدة
هاتف الموقع : ٨٣٨٣٩٨ ٤ (٩٧١)
فاكس الموقع : ٨٣٨٤٩٥ ٤ (٩٧١)
و ٨٣٨٥٧٧ ٤ (٩٧١)
رقم رخصة سلطة المنطقة الحرة لجبل علي ١٦٤٤

SALE SITE: P.O. Box 16897,
Jebel Ali Free Zone,
Dubai, United Arab Emirates
SITE PHONE: (971) 4 838398
SITE FAX: (971) 4 838495
OR (971) 4 838577
Jebel Ali Free Zone Authority Licence No. 1644

يتم بيع كل شئ الى مقدم أعلى عرض

EVERYTHING SELLS TO
THE HIGHEST BIDDER

just in time, sir, 400, four hundred thousand, 400, 410, 410, 410, now 420, 420, Jim are you there at 420? Four hundred and twenty

CHAPTER EIGHT: THE RIGHT RUNNING SHOES   105

put together after the Gulf region and its neighboring states were identified as a suitable area for a large auction."[26] Buyers from all over the Gulf, East Africa, India, Pakistan, Sri Lanka, and the Middle East spent $16 million at that auction.

"It was a two-day sale," remembered Randy Wall, who worked on the overseas team. "The night after the first day, a typhoon blew through, and it's extremely rare to have a storm like that in that part of the Middle East. We got into the yard the next morning, and the yard was flooded, and our tent was collapsed and blown down. So we just had to improvise, and away we went, selling on a stationary method."[27]

As the early 1990s ended, Ritchie Bros. could look with satisfaction on its program of international expansion. This rapid move across Europe and Asia and into the Middle East was accomplished using the same techniques that had worked so well in North America, and it was clear the company had changed forever. True to Dave Ritchie's oldest

Opposite and above: With outposts in Western Europe and Asia, Ritchie Bros. needed only to find a good Middle East location. In 1997, the company began staging sales in Dubai, United Arab Emirates. The first sale took a year to put together and attracted buyers from all over North Africa and the Indian subcontinent.

ambition, the Ritchie Bros. team had successfully established the world's first truly global industrial auction company.

Above: Listing day at the New York Stock Exchange, March 10, 1998. From left: Georges Ugeux, group executive vice president, New York Stock Exchange; Dave Ritchie, chairman and CEO, Ritchie Bros. Auctioneers; C. Russell Cmolik, then president and COO; Robert S. Armstrong, then manager, finance and corporate relations; and Peter J. Blake, then vice president, finance, and CFO.

Below: Five years later, on October 23, 2003, David Ritchie rings the Closing Bell at the Exchange to celebrate the company's 40th anniversary. From left: Rob Whitsit, senior vice president; Roger Rummel, senior vice president; NYSE representative; Randy Wall, president and COO; Dave Ritchie; Peter Blake, senior vice president and CFO; Russ Cmolik, director; Rob Mackay, executive vice president; and Bob Armstrong, vice president finance, corporate secretary.

CHAPTER NINE

THE FUTURE IS NOW

1997–PRESENT

*This business is still about tossing coins and guys making big deals.
That's where the fun is.*

—Dave Ritchie, 2002

BY THE LATE 1990s, Ritchie Bros. was indeed a very busy company. The promised technological revolution was in full bloom, and the company was introducing Internet services to enhance its live auctions. At the same time, the movement toward globalization had advanced rapidly in the 1990s after the communist Soviet Union collapsed, thus opening up more new markets. As North American commerce continued its steady advance around the globe, construction and building firms were never far behind the huge potential flow of money needed to fund new projects and infrastructure development.

Globally, used equipment value was estimated at $1 trillion toward the end of the decade, with an estimated $100 billion changing hands every year, and Ritchie Bros. looked forward to more growth, both through geographic expansion and by exploiting new technology.[1]

The Techno-Challenge

In 1997, the idea of using advanced communications technology to sell used equipment still had some maturing to do, however.

Traditionally, one of the major problems with remote bidding was a time lag during transmission. This complication plagued both satellite technology and the Internet. In a 60-second auction, where sales were completed in the blink of an eye, existing Internet tools weren't yet quick enough to keep pace with the fast-moving bidding. However, transmission capability had moved forward to the point that real-time bidding was possible using videoconferencing.

This was something Ritchie Bros. was interested in trying out. *Canadian Business* reporter Charles Mandel, in a 1997 article titled "Sale of the new machine," wrote:

Ritchie Bros. Auctioneers is probably the last company you would expect to find in cyberspace. The 40-year-old concern ... seems like a relic from the dinosaur age of business. But, stumbling into one of the remote Ritchie Bros. locations this past January, an unsuspecting

Even as Ritchie Bros. expanded internationally, it never changed its basic approach to auctioneering. Pictured is Don Chalmers, former Ritchie Bros. vice president, catching bids.

trailer is unused. Who'll give me twenty thousand? 20, 20, now twenty-two-five, two-five, two-five, and now twenty

108   THE LEGEND OF RITCHIE BROS. AUCTIONEERS

person might be forgiven for thinking he had encountered the Shopping Network crossed with Mission Impossible.[2]

What Mandel had witnessed was another industry first orchestrated by Ritchie Bros. Working from three cities in the United States, Ritchie Bros. had organized the first three-way video conferenced auction in December 1997.

"We're really excited about this video link," said the local manager for Ritchie Bros. "Customers will be able to attend the auction at their most convenient city. We're proud to make that first step in bringing industrial auctions into the high-tech world."[3]

The auction was a truck sale that had to be organized on very short notice and simultaneously broadcast in Missouri, Wisconsin, and Minnesota.

"There were probably 1,000 trucks and 2,500 trailers in about 30 areas of the Midwest, and they all had to come to three locations," said Frank McFadden, a Ritchie Bros. vice president at that time.[4]

With the equipment in place, the challenge was to link all three sites with video. To handle the task, Ritchie Bros. used a videoconferenc-

ing system with 52-inch screens at each location. The transmission allowed each audience to see its own bids, the equipment, and the other two audiences. The actual auction was conducted in St. Paul, but some of the larger buyers sent mechanics to each site to inspect the equipment.

This auction required careful coordination and tremendous resources, and while it wasn't the biggest auction that year, it was valuable proof that a video auction linking different locations was technologically feasible. But as many people remarked, the sale lacked some of the elements for which Ritchie Bros. had become famous.

"You're standing in this hotel ballroom with these huge video screens behind you," said McFadden. "You can't smell the diesel. You can't hear the engines or feel the vibrations."[5]

While the technology couldn't transmit exhaust fumes, it did allow buyers to see the other bidders, which Ritchie had assumed was important to assure everyone that the auction was truly unreserved. After the auction, however, Ritchie Bros. then–Marketing Manager Clay Tippett, who helped organize the sale, received mixed reviews.

"I remember talking to one older gentleman," Tippett said. "I asked, 'Did you like being able to see the customers?' He said he did as he'd never attended one of our auctions before and it built up his confidence to see the bidders at the other locations. Others in attendance who were longtime Ritchie Bros. customers said, 'We just want to see the numbers.' Because they knew us, they trusted us, and they knew it was an unreserved sale."[6]

Staging an auction using real-time video was pioneering in itself, but many people were already looking to the Internet for the future

Over 20 T/A Truck Tractors	**3 DAY** **Video Link** **UNRESERVED**
Over 300 S/A Truck Tractors	**rb Auction** Public **St. Paul, Minnesota** with participation by Video Link from Kansas City, Missouri and Clinton, Wisconsin
Over 1,600 Van Trailers	
Over 300 Jeeps & Dollies	**Tuesday, Dec. 16, 1997** (with Video Link) **Wednesday, Dec. 17, 1997** (with Video Link) **Thursday, Dec. 18, 1997** (St. Paul, MN only)
Over 90 Forklifts	**8:00 a.m. start each day** Information Line: (612) 639-1231 **RITCHIE BROS. Auctioneers** RITCHIE BROS. AUCTIONEERS INC. 821 COUNTY ROAD 27, BRIGHTON (DENVER), COLORADO 80601 TEL.: (303) 659-2962 FAX: (303) 659-2902 www.rbauction.com

This brochure advertised a three-city, video-linked auction. The event was the first of its kind staged in the heavy-equipment auction business and demonstrated the value of new communications technology.

five, 25, 25, twenty-seven-five, seven-five, and 30, 30, 30, now 31, 31, 32, 32, 32, Don, does your man want it? I need

CHAPTER NINE: THE FUTURE IS NOW   109

of auctioneering. Internet auctions were still a far cry from reality, however. Not only did the Internet lack the rumble of diesel engines and the smell of frying hamburgers, the existing technology wasn't fast enough to keep up with an auction.

Ritchie Bros. Goes Public

The company's expansion—in permanent sites, technology, and geography—was especially impressive considering that Ritchie Bros. remained a private company. But Ritchie Bros. had reached a critical stage in its growth and needed an infusion of capital to build new permanent facilities and continue its expansion around the globe. It was a fiercely independent company built mostly without going into debt, and the partners didn't like the idea of borrowing heavily. After decades of private ownership, in 1997 Ritchie Bros.' partners decided to take their company public.

Initially, the stock offering met with qualified enthusiasm among Canadian investment bankers. "They knew it would be successful," said Russ Cmolik. "But they were really in the air about what the value would be and how we would do it and how it would be accepted. They just didn't know exactly how it would be marketed and valued."[7]

In the midst of discussions with several Canadian banks, Ritchie Bros. contacted a Merrill Lynch banker based in Toronto, who called his colleagues in New York.

"They said, 'Get after them,'" Cmolik remembered. "They knew about us because they have analysts specifically following the heavy-construction equipment industry, and they had also followed some of the distributors and been to our auctions and were very familiar with the name. Other American bankers got all over us very rapidly, and we went to New York and we sat from 7 A.M. until 9 P.M. with investment bankers who were coming in to make presentations to us to get in on the deal."[8]

On February 13, 1998, Ritchie Bros. filed a registration statement with the Securities and

Upon hearing that Richie Bros. wanted to go public, some investment bankers wondered how the company would be accepted by Wall Street. They needn't have worried. The company's shares started trading higher than expected, giving Ritchie Bros.—and those investment bankers who had been wise enough to get in on the deal—cause for celebration.

Exchange Commission for a proposed initial offering of 2.9 million shares of common stock to be listed on the New York Stock Exchange. The offering was led by New York–based Merrill Lynch, with Furman Selz and Morgan Stanley as comanagers. Initially, the financial community expected Ritchie Bros.' stock to be priced between $14 and $16 a share.

On the day of the offering, the *Vancouver Sun* reported that Ritchie Bros. made "a stunning debut."[9] The shares were priced at $17, and trading opened above $21 under the symbol RBA on the New York Stock Exchange. The significantly oversubscribed IPO raised $49.3 million, most of which was earmarked for

Bob Brawley, right, and Frank McFadden retained significant roles after the Ritchie Bros. IPO. Brawley was a vice president in the U.S. operation, and McFadden was a senior valuation analyst, helping field representatives bid on packages of equipment.

expanding the company's network of auction sites.[10] After the offering, Ritchie Bros. had 16.1 million shares outstanding and a market capitalization of $340.4 million.[11]

"I came away flabbergasted at the franchise these people have built," said Sebastian Van Berkom, president of Van Berkom and Associates Inc. of Montreal, who bought Ritchie stock for a fund his company manages. "This isn't a capital-intensive business. Their main resource is basically a kind of intellectual property."[12]

The company also received praise from then-analyst David O'Neill of William Blair & Company in Chicago, who said, "It's one of the greatest financial formulas I've ever seen. No matter what statistics you look at—operating margin, return on assets, incremental margin or whatever—this company would be a four-star performer on its income statement."[13]

Although the company had been closely held for so long, going public didn't drastically change it, said Cmolik.

It's not been difficult. In some respects, going through the IPO process was healthy because we had to actually sit down and write down a lot of things that we intuitively knew. We had to put in writing, both from a theoretical point of view and a legal point of view: "This is what we do, and this is what our philosophies are." It makes you reevaluate them.[14]

The public offering also allowed Ritchie Bros. to acknowledge the years of hard work by its employees. When the company was still preparing to go public, the partners wanted to give 5 percent of the value of the company to Ritchie Bros. staff.

"The investment bankers told us not to," Cmolik said. "They said, 'Every company that is doing an IPO says the same thing, but one of the reasons they don't, particularly international companies, is because it's too complicated legally.' But we followed through. Our employees are the company."[15]

In the end, employees at Ritchie Bros. were given stock that was soon worth a total of more than $25 million.

A Year of Transition: Breaking the $1 Billion Barrier

The infusion of capital allowed Ritchie Bros. to embark on an expansion program that lasted for the next five years and dwarfed anything the company had ever engineered. In the first 24 months following the public offering, permanent sites were opened in Perris, California; Brisbane, Australia; Atlanta, Georgia; Moerdijk, the Netherlands; Bolton, Ontario; Morris, Illinois; Montreal, Quebec; and Singapore.

In the midst of this expansion, Ritchie Bros. was struck by tragedy when Mark Clarke died suddenly in early 1998. Clarke, who had been running Ritchie's operation in Europe, had contributed greatly to the company's successful push overseas and was much admired throughout the company. Subsequently, Randy Wall moved from Canada to the Netherlands as the new managing director, Europe and the Middle East.

While the company still mourned, 1998 passed in a flurry of new facility openings and huge sales, including the largest sale until that time in North America. The Fort Worth, Texas, auction on March 11–12, 1998, produced gross sales in excess of $30 million. This milestone occurred two days after Ritchie Bros. celebrated its 35th anniversary of industrial auctioneering

Right: When it came time to open a permanent site in Europe, Ritchie Bros. selected the port of Moerdijk in the Netherlands. This yard attracted equipment and buyers from all over Europe and provided easy access to international shipping. The site would soon host some of the largest sales in auction history.

Below: Guylain Turgeon, managing director for Europe, catches bids at a Ritchie Bros. auction. Reflecting a corporate culture of "everyone works, everyone contributes," it is common to see Ritchie Bros. executives catching bids.

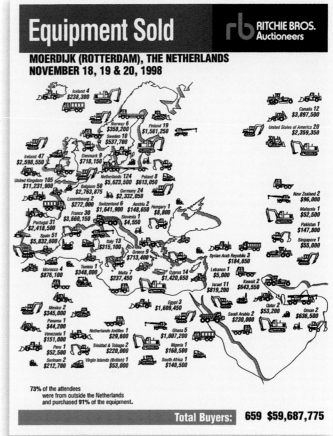

Equipment Sold — RITCHIE BROS. Auctioneers

MOERDIJK (ROTTERDAM), THE NETHERLANDS
NOVEMBER 18, 19 & 20, 1998

Iceland 4 $238,300
Canada 12 $3,897,500
United States of America 20 $2,359,350
Norway 6 $358,200
Finland 19 $1,561,250
Sweden 10 $537,700
Ireland 47 $2,598,550
Denmark 9 $718,150
United Kingdom 105 $11,231,900
Netherlands 124 $5,623,500
Poland 8 $613,050
New Zealand 2 $96,000
Belgium 50 $2,763,875
Germany 24 $2,332,050
Malaysia 1 $52,500
Luxembourg 2 $272,000
Switzerland 6 $1,641,900
Austria 2 $148,650
Hungary 1 $8,800
Pakistan 1 $147,800
France 30 $3,660,150
Slovenia 1 $4,550
Singapore 1 $55,000
Portugal 31 $2,418,500
Spain 51 $5,832,600
Italy 13 $315,100
Syrian Arab Republic 3 $184,650
Greece 9 $713,400
Morocco 4 $876,100
Tunisia 1 $348,000
Malta 7 $237,450
Cyprus 14 $1,420,650
Lebanon 4 $5,000
Israel 11 $819,200
Kuwait 2 $643,550
Qatar 2 $53,200
Oman 2 $636,500
Egypt 3 $1,609,450
Saudi Arabia 2 $230,000
Mexico 2 $345,900
Panama 1 $44,200
Venezuela 1 $151,000
Netherlands Antilles 1 $29,600
Ghana 5 $1,007,200
Nigeria 1 $168,500
Peru 1 $52,500
Trinidad & Tobago 2 $220,000
Surinam 2 $212,700
Virgin Islands (British) 1 $53,000
South Africa 1 $140,500

73% of the attendees were from outside the Netherlands and purchased 91% of the equipment.

Total Buyers: 659 $59,687,775

at a reception in Toronto. That June, another Fort Worth auction grossed $27 million.

The very first sale at the new facility in Atlanta, in April 1999, grossed $18.2 million.

A three-day sale in Rotterdam in March 1998, with bidders from 62 countries, grossed more than $45.8 million. This record was broken in June by a $48.9 million sale, also in Rotterdam, which was soon bested in turn by a three-day sale that grossed $59 million. Even for a seasoned employee like Rob Mackay, then vice president, Asia-Pacific, the size and depth of the sale "blew us away." Mackay recalls looking down over row upon row of more than 400 excavators and telling Dave Ritchie, "I think we may have overdone it here!"

Randy Wall, still new in his position of managing director, Europe and the Middle East, helped manage this huge undertaking, which was complicated by the fact that Ritchie Bros. was in the middle of building a new auction site at Moerdijk, the Netherlands.

"It was the first sale on our new site in Moerdijk and my second sale after coming over here," he said. "We were in the midst of construction of this new facility, and the site work was still under way. So it was messy, combined with record flooding in northwestern Europe. The conditions were nasty, but after it was all said and done, it was a tremendous success. The amount of effort and the teamwork that went into it was astounding, and it sure made you feel good."[16]

A sale in Olympia, Washington, generated $21.1 million in September 1998.

Sales at Dubai in 1998 totaled $65 million. True to predictions, the Dubai auction site had quickly established itself as a hub for business throughout the Middle East although its opening wasn't without mishap.

"For the grand opening, we gave speeches and had photo ops and so on," remembered Russ Cmolik.

This auction brochure advertises the March 1998 sale in Dubai. The site grew quickly, with total gross sales of about $65 million in its first full year.

And they brought this great big cake out. It was about 9 o'clock at night, a beautiful night outside on the lawn at the hotel. Somebody from our staff brings out a wire mesh cage of pigeons—we didn't know anything about it because it was a surprise.

But it turns out that these pigeons had been in this cage for three days, and they were all cramped and looking a little limp. I don't even know if pigeons fly at night, but when they opened up the cage, none of them flew out.[17]

Near the end of the year, in November 1998, Ritchie Bros. crossed the $1 billion mark in annual gross auction sales with a sale at Fort Worth. That same month, the company registered its 1.5 millionth bidder.

"Ritchie Bros. is the envy of the auctioneering world, with a superb balance sheet, steady growth and solid profits," wrote reporter David Steinhart in the *Financial Post.* The same article quoted analyst Dan Dykens as saying, "This is a company that does everything right. It has no peers and continues to have high margins."[18]

By the end of 1998, Ritchie Bros. was larger than its next 40 competitors combined. It was three times larger than its nearest competitor, Forke Brothers, and still growing quickly.[19]

The Amalgamation of Giants

Never an acquisitive company, Ritchie Bros. had always preferred to grow from within and enjoyed its independence. It didn't like to borrow money, and it didn't like to take on partners for auction packages. Despite its worldwide reach, Ritchie Bros. had retained the distinctive close-knit culture of its early years. But as it expanded its role as the leader in industrial auctions, Ritchie Bros. thought it made financial and business sense to consider an acquisition.

The strategy was driven in part by growing consolidation in the auction business. In the early 1990s, after watching Ritchie Bros.

209. These are fine trucks, rigged right and ready to roll. High bidder has choice—take one, two, or take all three.

CHAPTER NINE: THE FUTURE IS NOW   113

Above: Forke Brothers began its auction career selling livestock in Nebraska in the 1930s. The company later moved into industrial equipment auctions.

Below: Before Ritchie Bros. built its new facilities, most company auctions were conducted outdoors.

move into the U.S. market, Randy Ringhaver at Ring Power Corporation decided to "get into the auction business." A major Caterpillar dealer, he approached Caterpillar and "told them how the auction industry was taking over the used-equipment market and that Caterpillar needs to sit up and pay attention to this because the redistribution of used equipment was changing quite rapidly into the hands of one person, Dave Ritchie."[20]

Consequently, Ringhaver got permission from Caterpillar to develop an auction company that would be owned by Caterpillar dealers. He soon partnered with another Caterpillar dealer named De Thompson, who was based in Nashville, Tennessee, and they bought Forke Brothers, one of the largest U.S. auction companies and the closest thing to true competition that Ritchie Bros. had.

Founded in 1921 in Nebraska by brothers Herb and Al Forke, the company held its first auction in Lincoln, Nebraska, selling livestock and farm equipment. In the 1930s, during the Great Depression and the dust bowl in the farming belt, Forke Brothers participated in the "penny auctions" of foreclosed farms and equipment. After World War II, the company began to specialize in industrial auctions.

Ringhaver remembered negotiating the final details of the sale with the eight Forke Brothers, when the partners adjourned to a private meeting. They left Ringhaver sitting outside the conference room with his attorney. He heard the telephone begin to ring, and since it continued ringing and no one was around to answer it, Ringhaver went in and picked up the phone. Dave Ritchie was on the other end.

Let's start low. Who'll give me fifty thousand, 50, 50, 50 for choice, gentlemen, 50, 50, now 60, now 70, now 80, 80, 80

114   THE LEGEND OF RITCHIE BROS. AUCTIONEERS

"He was asking for the Forke manager, Rob Whitsit," Ringhaver remembered. "And I said, 'Well, Rob's in a meeting. This is Randy. What can I do for you, Dave?' Dave asked me what I was doing out there, and I said, 'Well, I guess I'm getting in the auction business.' He just said, 'Oh my! That's interesting.' He must have said 'That's interesting' about ten times."[21]

The acquisition of Forke Brothers by the Cat dealers proceeded, and Ringhaver soon started offering minimum guarantees through Forke Brothers, something the company had never attempted before.

Ringhaver was now in direct competition with Ritchie Bros. The big Florida sales, for example, which had quickly become a staple in the auction industry, were no longer staged by Ritchie Bros.

With competition organizing so quickly, Dave Ritchie naturally was interested in working something out with Ringhaver almost from their first conversation. Shortly after the Forke acquisition, Ritchie called Ringhaver to

say, "I'd like to make you an offer on this company. You don't want this aggravation. You've got a great life down there in the equipment business and going fishing on the weekends."

But Ringhaver wasn't interested. The partners were still flush with the enthusiasm of the new acquisition and began laying plans to rapidly scale up the business. Before long, however, the newly minted auctioneers found that Dave Ritchie had indeed been correct.

"Little did we know that it was going to become very capital intensive," Ringhaver said.

We had to buy all these damn facilities and do guarantees and buy equipment and so on and so forth. When we got into it, we felt like we were bringing a lot of clout and capital into the company and that we were going to get all these Caterpillar dealers in the United States to join forces with us. Unfortunately, we made a limited offering to all the Caterpillar dealers, which took us about six months and a couple hundred thousand dollars, and right in the mid-

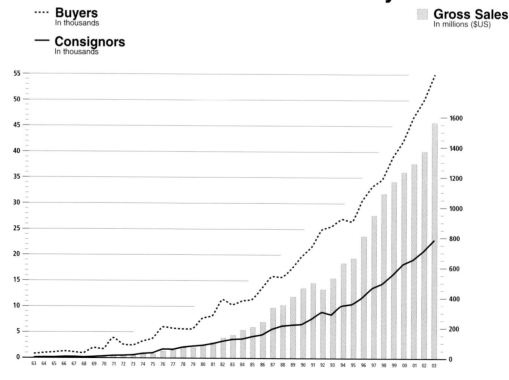

Ritchie Bros. Growth History

thousand, 80, 80, I'm bid 70, need 80, 80... these are 1997 models, gentlemen, 80 thousand, OK I'll do 75, 75, 75, now 80,

CHAPTER NINE: THE FUTURE IS NOW   115

Rob Whitsit came to Ritchie Bros. as vice president of the big Southeast division after being general manager of Forke Brothers.

dle of it, Caterpillar came out with a statement saying they didn't approve of Caterpillar dealers being in the auction business.[22]

With the rug effectively pulled out from underneath them, Ringhaver and his partners were forced to consider their options. They considered a public offering and also set up a meeting with Dave Ritchie, but nothing came of it, and Forke continued to build aggressively.

Forke next made a bid for Europe and beat out Ritchie Bros. for a lucrative deal. "I was pushing very hard for the deal and made a very, very high offer on it," Cmolik said. "But they leapfrogged us and took this deal. They'd never had an auction before in Europe."[23]

Although the Forke sale in Rotterdam grossed $20 million, it did not measure up to their expectations, and pretty soon Ringhaver found himself talking to Cmolik. "I told him that if we were going to make a marriage of these companies somehow, we'd better be talking about it sooner rather than later," Cmolik said. "We're going one way down the road, and you're going another, and it's going to be tougher the more time that goes by."[24]

Serious discussions began in late 1998, a year when Forke Brothers generated record sales. Throughout negotiations, the two companies circled around each other. Dave Ritchie would ask how much Ringhaver wanted. "I'd throw out a number like $100 million," Ringhaver said. "Then Dave would laugh and hoot and holler and say he could buy a lot of businesses more profitable than we were for that." Finally, after several starts and stops, the two met in an airport hangar in Tampa and shook hands. That was when Ringhaver knew the acquisition was going through.

"I knew that when I shook hands with Dave in principle we had a deal, that even if other people couldn't agree on certain things,

80, now 85, 85, 85 and 90, 90 thousand, 90, 90, 90. Dave, does your man want one more shot? He's been with us all the

116   THE LEGEND OF RITCHIE BROS. AUCTIONEERS

Dave and I would be able to get back together," Ringhaver said.[25]

The deal was closed on April 1, 1999. To buy the Forke Brothers auction business, Ritchie Bros. paid $25 million cash, plus 100,000 shares of Ritchie Bros. stock and warrants for 400,000 more shares. The company paid an additional $12 million for land, buildings, and other capital assets such as permanent auction sites in Albuquerque, New Mexico; Statesville, North Carolina; Fort Worth, Texas; and Ocala, Florida.

Forke's head offices in Lincoln, Nebraska, replaced the Denver office as Ritchie Bros.' U.S. headquarters, and Forke General Manager Rob Whitsit joined Ritchie Bros. "After seeing the quality of people that they had there, we decided that instead of consolidating everything more and more into Richmond, British Columbia, it would be an ideal time to open up an administrative office in the United States," Cmolik said.[26]

Forke's North Carolina and New Mexico locations were new auction sites for Ritchie. The Florida site was put in service, and Texas, which was redundant, was mothballed. With the new facilities, the combined Ritchie Bros. operation included 22 auction sites: 13 in the United States, six in Canada, and one each in Europe, Australia, and the Middle East.

For his part, Ringhaver was not entirely out of the auction business following the acquisition. Although he had sold the auction operation, for a short while he maintained a finance company called Forke Credit, which was soon renamed FCC Equipment Financing and subsequently sold to Caterpillar Financial Services Corporation. Dave Ritchie agreed to cooperate with the new company, which would soon advertise in Ritchie Bros. brochures and have a presence at Ritchie Bros. auctions.

The Internet:
Auction Tool of the Future?

With the burst of new facilities, the acquisition of Forke Brothers, and the steady increase in the number of salespeople, it might have

been tempting for Ritchie Bros. to rest on its laurels as it headed into the new millennium. It had continued to expand rapidly, especially overseas, even while negotiating with Forke. In 1999, new offices opened in Moerdijk, the Netherlands, and Brisbane, Australia, and the company purchased land in Baltimore, Maryland, and Montreal, Quebec.[27]

Soon, new sales offices were opened in Hong Kong, Spain, Italy, Austria, South Africa, Saudi Arabia, and Jordan. "We are very pleased with the pace of our international expansion," commented Dave Ritchie in a press release. "We are continually working hard to expand our reach and to deliver a global marketplace to our customers."[28]

Yet realistically, with only a fraction of the global used-equipment market, Ritchie Bros. was surrounded by competitive pressures and always looking for a leg up. Like most companies in the late 1990s, Ritchie Bros. was closely watching the growth of the Internet to see how it could take advantage of the technology to enhance its business and improve customer service. In 1999 Ritchie Bros. once again used ConExpo to broadcast via video-conferencing from its Olympia auction into its booth at the Las Vegas trade show. Bids were relayed by telephone back to the auctioneer. During the two-day event, more than $1 million worth of trucks and construction equipment

RITCHIE BROS.
LOCATIONS IN 2000

○ Sales Offices
● Permanent Auction Sites
◌ Regional Auction Units

was sold to buyers in Las Vegas. New Internet services were also introduced, including on-line consignments and on-line proxy bidding.[29]

This was progress, but it still represented only a fraction of Ritchie Bros. sales. And the culture of the used-equipment business was still not ready to accept the Internet.

"Is the Internet going to be the Holy Grail of the way used equipment gets sold?" asked Peter Blake, Ritchie Bros.' chief financial officer, in 2000. "I think the jury is still out. It's probably not the nirvana way of buying and selling used equipment, but if it turns out that way, we will be there leading the charge."[30]

The Ritchie Bros. team continued to experiment with technology. Early in 2000, a sale in Florida was broadcast over the Internet as it was happening, kicking off a schedule of live broadcasts from selected Ritchie Bros. facilities. These initial broadcasts offered a view-only service without bidding capability.

"We're anticipating that our auction broadcasts will interest many construction equipment owners," said Clay Tippett, then marketing manager. "By broadcasting auctions on our Web site, customers are able to view the auction

With capital from the IPO, Ritchie Bros. embarked on an aggressive program of building permanent auction yards. In March 2000, the company celebrated a grand opening of a facility in Morris, Illinois, above. Later that year (below), Peter Blake, chief financial officer, and Doug Olive, Prairie Region regional manager, visited the construction site of a new facility in Nisku, just outside of Edmonton, Alberta.

and watch equipment being sold into a global marketplace, even if they can't attend in person. The number of customers on our mailing list who use the Internet is growing, . . . so it makes sense that we show them our auctions on the Internet."[31]

But the basic issues remained the same: each piece of used equipment was unique, and most buyers needed to see a machine in person to feel comfortable with it.

"The technology is moving forward really fast, and our information technology and marketing groups are continuously looking at innovation and research," said Ed Banser, then vice president of the South Central United States Division. "When we do get there, it'll probably increase our business to some extent, but the guys who come to buy a Caterpillar tractor still like to see it, touch it, and kick it. We believe that's still going to be the guts of the auction business."[32]

John Ivester, former owner of *Last Bid*, a trade magazine that published the sales results of auctions worldwide, had followed the industry for 30 years and agreed that auctions attract a special breed of buyer.

"It's the nature of the business," Ivester said. "If you're paying $50,000 or $100,000 or $200,000 for a piece of iron, you're going to want to look at the equipment. I could see how

that price? He takes them all! Of course he does! Three times the money. Wrap 'em up, put a bow on 'em and

CHAPTER NINE: THE FUTURE IS NOW   119

brand-new equipment would sell because that's like buying an airplane ticket. If you're going to the same place at the same time, there's no difference. But for used iron, there's a big difference in where it's at, the condition of it, and the appearance of it."[33]

Nevertheless, the Internet continued to develop as a powerful tool. In 2000, for instance, Ritchie Bros. introduced an on-line service called rbauctionRe$ults that allowed customers to research historic equipment prices, finding out how much a certain piece of equipment had sold for at a Ritchie Bros. auction.

This new service generated a great deal of internal discussion among Ritchie Bros.' executives, remembered Bob Armstrong, vice president of Internet services. On the one hand, increasing transparency was creating a more efficient market and this was very positive for the company. On the other hand, there was a concern that this increased access to Ritchie Bros. data could help the competition. As it turned out, however, rbauctionRe$ults was an "absolute success."

"People started using the information available on the Ritchie Bros. Web site as a source

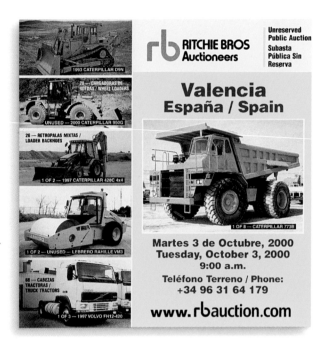

Throughout 2000, Ritchie Bros. celebrated more big international sales. Above, an auction brochure advertises a sale in Valencia, Spain, while below, bidder/buyer maps from sales in Dubai, Valencia, and Fort Worth reflect the tremendous geographic reach of a Ritchie Bros. auction; it is not unusual to have buyers from three or four continents at a single sale.

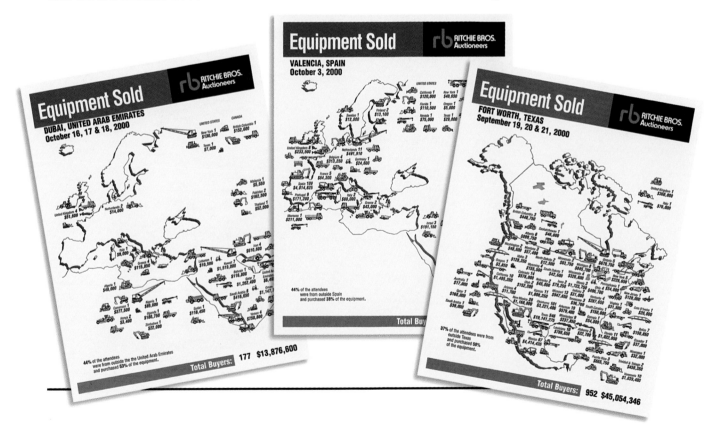

of knowledge, or benchmark, for what was happening in the world," Armstrong said, helping to solidify the company's reputation as the authoritative source for information about the used truck and equipment markets.[34]

The next step, called rbauctionBid-Live, was officially unveiled in March 2002, and it represented the culmination of two years of careful work. For the first time, Ritchie Bros. would begin accepting bids over the Internet. Although it was widely agreed that the Internet would never replace the "kick the tires" mentality of the auction business, Ritchie Bros. had determined there was a place for it—providing, of course, that the two main concerns about Internet auctions could be settled. The first was related to security, making sure that bidders were authentic and the company could

In 2000, Ritchie Bros. celebrated the opening of a new auction yard in Dubai, United Arab Emirates. The region steadily gained in importance and by the turn of the millennium had emerged as the sought-after hub for all the Middle East.

time! We've got lot number 555, triple nickel. It's a loader, knee-deep in rubber. Start me off. Who'll give me one hun-

CHAPTER NINE: THE FUTURE IS NOW   121

Above: The Ritchie Bros. Web site bid window during an auction. Through its Web site, Ritchie Bros. was able to expand its pool of potential buyers.

Left: Sylvain Touchette, left, shakes hands with Russ Cmolik. In 2002, Touchette was the vice president of Ritchie Bros.' Eastern Canada Division.

still prohibit customer buybacks. The second was integrating the Internet into the normal Ritchie Bros. auction without disrupting the fast-paced flow of events.

The rbauctionBid-Live system took care of both. A rigorous registration process ensured that only legitimate bidders were able to participate. These qualified Internet bidders followed the auctioneer's call, live and in real time, thanks to a system that delivered real-time bid and ask-price information and images of the items being sold. When an Internet bidder clicked his bid button, the on-line bid was transmitted to the auction site in real time. The auctioneer simply treated Internet bids like any other bid from the audience.

"We still have thousands of people attending the live auctions," Armstrong said. "We haven't affected the live auction experience. We've enhanced it. By the end of 2002, Internet bidders were the buyer or runner-up on over 10 percent of the lots being offered on-line. The rbauctionBid-Live service was already creating real value for our customers."[35]

Perhaps best of all, Ritchie Bros. soon realized it wasn't cannibalizing its existing audience. Rather, through the Internet, Ritchie Bros. was extending the auction option to people who otherwise might have missed sales. In fact, the company had achieved more than $70 million in sales to Internet bidders by the end of 2002. The year 2003 got off to an even better start: by the end of the third quarter, Ritchie Bros. had broken $100 million in sales to Internet bidders. In one Fort Worth auction that summer, Internet bidders purchased a record-breaking $8.3 million of trucks and equipment.

Marching On

Throughout these important years, the company continued to hold big sales and bring in big revenue. In 1999, sales hit more than $1.1 billion. That year, a three-day sale in Fort Worth

dred thousand dollars? Who'll bid 100, 1... 1... 100, 100, 100, you know it'll get there, 100, 1... 1... 100 thousand! Let's go

122   THE LEGEND OF RITCHIE BROS. AUCTIONEERS

Mike Ritchie, who is vice president, Western Canada Division as well as Ken Ritchie's son and Dave Ritchie's nephew, started working for Ritchie Bros. in 1979. He became a partner in 1996.

set a new record for North America with a gross of $37.5 million.

Soon after, because of the Forke Brothers acquisition, Ritchie Bros. staged its first auction for Ring Power in more than five years. Held in Ocala, Florida, in early 2000, the auction produced good results. However, Ritchie Bros. wasn't immediately satisfied, remembered Bob Leavy, then regional manager of the Florida operation.

"Dave called us and said, 'What do we need to make this thing work?'" Leavy remembered. "And we all knew. We said, 'We need to get back to Orlando. We need to have better exposure.' "[36]

Dave agreed and told the team to find a new piece of property in Orlando and he would "build a world-class auction facility." Shortly afterward, Leavy found 136 acres owned by the University of Florida. The property was near two major highways and an airport and was only 20 minutes from the internationally famous Disney resorts. Dave flew down, fell in love with the property, and bought it. The new Orlando yard was soon under construction, and even before the grand opening in 2002, it was hosting big auctions.

Besides the Orlando yard, new facilities were under construction in Phoenix, Arizona; Edmonton, Alberta; and Prince George, British Columbia. The Edmonton yard had the distinction of being Ritchie Bros.' first double-ramp yard, meaning the company could auction an astounding 3,000 lots a day. In this way, Ritchie Bros. hoped to compress its traditional two-day sale into a single day, a huge convenience for customers. Shortly after its grand opening, the yard hosted the largest auction in Canadian history and one of the largest in company history.

In 2001, still following the strategy mapped out during its IPO, Ritchie Bros. posted strong gross auction sales of just under $1.3 billion and a whopping 28 percent increase in income. "[We were] carrying on with the design that we started when we took the company public," noted Peter Blake, chief financial officer. "That meant building the platform for growth by adding facilities, infrastructure, and people. At the end of 2001, we had around 195 sales guys."[37]

September 11, 2001

Ritchie Bros. was in the middle of a very successful year in 2001 when tragedy struck on September 11. On that day, terrorists hijacked four planes and flew three of them into targets in New York City and Washington, D.C. The fourth crashed in a field in Pennsylvania. In all, nearly 3,000 people from more than 50 countries were killed, the World Trade Center was destroyed, and the Pentagon was damaged. In the week

with 70, 70, 70 thousand... 70... 70... 7... 7... 7... 70, c'mon gentlemen, I can't start the auction. You have to start it.

CHAPTER NINE: THE FUTURE IS NOW 123

after those attacks, Ritchie Bros. took the extra-ordinary step of rescheduling three auctions. Dave Ritchie was at one of the yards and had the difficult task of informing 200 buyers already on-site for the planned auction the following day that the sale had been postponed because of the international tragedy. Despite the inconvenience, there was not a single complaint.

The auction industry was more fortunate than many businesses. In the long run, the attacks and the subsequent global recession had no negative impact on Ritchie Bros.' business. The first post-attack sale was held a week later in Ohio, and the company was pleased to see that it was very much business as usual. Even the sales in Dubai, United Arab Emirates, were unaffected: As a staunch American and European ally, Dubai was a safe haven in a sea of unrest. By 2002, Ritchie Bros. was staging three auctions a year in the oil-rich Arab emirate, including a June auction that ran at night to avoid the 120-degree daytime heat.

"It's a tremendous success," said Stephen Branch, who ran the 20-person Ritchie Bros. operation in Dubai in 2002. "We start at 4 P.M. and go to about 11 o'clock. Afterward, we have a traditional Middle East meal and celebration."[38]

Part of the reason the Dubai office has been so successful, according to Branch, is

A new 125-acre auction site was opened in Nisku (Edmonton), Alberta, in June 2002. The facility featured dual auction ramps, allowing Ritchie Bros. to sell more items per day.

124   THE LEGEND OF RITCHIE BROS. AUCTIONEERS

the Arab community's traditional comfort with bartering.

"In the Arab culture, there's no such thing as a fixed price, the difference being, of course, that in an auction, the bids are going up," Branch said.

When you're haggling, you're trying to bring the bids down. The biggest problem I saw when I first came here was they would get the bid, then they came up and wanted to negotiate the price. Then they were ready to bargain. They didn't realize they had already done that process. But now they've gotten used to our way of auctioning, and it's fit really well.[39]

Keeping That "Secondhand Sense"

By 2002, Ritchie Bros. had grown beyond even the most optimistic expectations of the three brothers from Kelowna who had founded the company almost 40 years before. Over the previous four years, the company had spent about $150 million building auction facilities and had increased its sales force by 70 percent. Ritchie Bros. had offices in 21 countries, including 26 auction sites, and the company staged more than 120 auctions annually.

The Texas territory, Ritchie Bros.' largest in the United States, also continued to evolve. In 2002, Ed Banser announced his retirement. Nick Nicholson, who had actually begun his career with Ritchie Bros. as the first sales representative in Houston, was chosen to succeed Banser. Nicholson had been managing the Great Lakes region, but it had long been his hope to run the company's giant Texas operation.

"When Eddie Banser hired me in 1987, he said, 'What are your aspirations? What would you like to do in the company?'" Nicholson remembered. "I looked at him and said, 'I'd

Nick Nicholson joined Ritchie Bros. wanting to someday run the giant Texas operation. Fourteen years later, he succeeded Ed Banser as vice president leading the South Central region.

like your job! I want to work up.' He laughed and that was that."[40]

The customer service department, comprised of a handful of full-time employees, tracked some 350,000 customers all over the world, keeping a current list of buyers and sellers that represented one of Ritchie Bros.' most potent competitive advantages. "Their exposure for equipment for sale is second to none," said Don Breen, a senior vice president with Industrial Construction Group and longtime customer. "My equipment had better exposure, and the market advice that we got from Ritchie in terms of how to sell the equipment was very, very educational."[41]

The marketing department, meanwhile, advertised sales in publications all over the

9... 90 thousand, thank you! Now 1... 1... 100, bid 100, 100 thousand dollars, now up 5—105, 105, one more time 105, now

CHAPTER NINE: THE FUTURE IS NOW   125

Above: Rob Mackay was named executive vice president of Ritchie Bros. in 2002, after Russ Cmolik announced his retirement. Mackay had been senior vice president–operations.

Right: Stephen Branch, right, poses with his father. Branch moved his family to Dubai to run the company's large auction operation there. To beat the desert heat, Ritchie Bros. now sometimes conducts its summer auctions at night.

equipment and make sure the company never lost its all-important "secondhand sense."

In 2002, while closing in on $1.4 billion in annual gross auction sales, Ritchie Bros. was still looking for growth opportunities. In May, Ritchie Bros. announced the acquisition of All Peace Auctions, a northern Alberta auctioneer that specialized in industrial and agricultural equipment. The acquisition included a permanent auction site of more than 30 acres in Grande Prairie, Alberta, and helped expand sales of agriculture equipment.

Ritchie Bros. has truly become a large company, a fact that wasn't without its bittersweet moments. Dave Ritchie, the company's chairman and CEO, remained the most visible symbol of Ritchie Bros.' unique operating culture. After so many years, Dave Ritchie had become known around the world. It was even an insider's joke at Ritchie Bros. that buyers all over the globe looking for a favor would remark, "I'm a personal friend of Dave Ritchie's."

world, mailed out more than 10 million auction brochures annually, appeared at trade shows, distributed promotional items, prepared multimedia presentations, handled e-mail and Internet relationship initiatives, and helped with research and data mining. Also, an entire department of people, headed by Gary Caufield and Helen Menges, ensured that Ritchie Bros. lived up to its pledge of a free-and-clear title on everything it sold and followed up on the legal aspects of the sales.

When it came to actually bidding on packages of equipment, Ritchie Bros. faced one of its greatest challenges, but it could also call on one of its greatest strengths, its sophisticated risk management system. The company relied on senior valuation analysts to help the field representatives bid successfully on packages of

But elsewhere in the company, Ritchie Bros. was changing. In the summer of 2002, longtime leader Russ Cmolik announced his retirement as president and chief operating officer. His departure created a ripple effect of promotions throughout the company. Randy Wall, while retaining his responsibility for operations in Europe and the Middle East, was named to the position of president and COO. At the same time, Rob Mackay was promoted to executive vice president, assuming responsibility for the company's U.S. operations as well as retaining responsibility for the Asia, Australia, and South America operations; Peter Blake became senior vice president, in addition to his role as chief financial officer; Roger Rummel and Rob Whitsit were promoted to senior vice presidents. Together with Dave Ritchie, these leaders formed the newly established Executive Committee of Ritchie Bros.

Looking back on his long career with Ritchie Bros., Cmolik could rightfully be satisfied with its record of growth and unique legacy in the used equipment business. "I've had a fantastic run, and I guess I'm most fiercely proud of the people and the organization we've put together," Cmolik said.

In 2002, Randy Wall was named president and chief operating officer of Ritchie Bros. after Russ Cmolik announced his retirement.

Going back a long ways, the key players were the three Ritchie brothers and the old partners. Dave Ritchie was, of course, the pivotal guy. He had a lot of the vision and the view. I'm very much a business guy. My part of the organization was growing and developing the internal organization, the people, the management, the systems, and support. But I loved getting out with the customers as much as anybody. It's the most fun part of the business, for sure.[42]

Not least of all, Cmolik had helped create a team that could seamlessly continue building Ritchie Bros. around the world.

"He has built a management team that is ready to step up to the plate and take this company forward," said Dave Ritchie.

As the largest company in a unique field, Ritchie Bros. always faced the challenge of finding good people. Ritchie Bros. employees needed to understand auctioneering, heavy equipment, contracting, and global operations yet not be afraid of getting down in the mud and working in the yards. People like this were hard to find outside of the company, so Ritchie Bros. had to train its own leaders, and this is where Russ Cmolik's legacy will "undoubtedly lie," according to Dave Ritchie.

"I have always viewed the development of our young managers as my number one respon-

get him, Rob! Your guy's out! 113, sir! Last call 113, thank you! Now 114, 114, now 115, 115, 116! 117—a two-way race here! 117

CHAPTER NINE: THE FUTURE IS NOW   127

sibility," Cmolik said. "Watching them grow into leaders has been the best part of my job."

I can tell you I'm a proud guy to stand up here and tell you we've done a great job of it. We've got a management team in place, both at the head office and in the field, that is the strongest team we've ever fielded. The breadth and depth of ability that we have here is outstanding, and they're mostly young folks. We've got a couple of good old-timers that have the experience and can lead the company at the very highest level, but beyond that, there's plenty of bench strength. It's a lot of young people combined with a lot of experience.[43]

Ritchie Bros. remained headquartered in Richmond, British Columbia, operating from a new head office building. It had grown beyond a family operation to one that relied on the contributions of loyal employees who were willing to travel the world looking for good packages of equipment. It had become a public company, responsible for generating quarterly reports and educating investors and analysts, who had gained an appreciation for Ritchie Bros.' unique business model.

While Ritchie Bros. wore these outward symbols of change with pride, in many important ways it had not changed at all from the company founded by a group of rowdy brothers who scoured western Canada for sawmill deals. Its auctions were still unreserved, and the company was still driven by the goal of providing superior customer service. Although it had spawned a generation of imitators, Ritchie Bros. was still known as the honest auctioneer, and its equipment still rumbled over its trademark ramp. Most importantly, the principles laid out four decades before continued to attract and retain both lifelong employees and lifelong customers.

"This business is all about strong relationships," said Don Chalmers, former vice president of Ritchie Bros.' original territory in western Canada. "People in the equipment business see Dave Ritchie as being totally accessible, knowledgeable, hardworking, entrepreneurial, and very generous in spirit, as well as in fact," he said.[44]

As closely as he is associated with the company, Dave Ritchie himself was always the first to point out that Ritchie Bros. owed its success to the talented team of people who worked there. From its first days, Ritchie Bros. had been run by consensus, and it was built on the integrity of its people and its steadfast dedication to customers.

"Our customers are a unique group," Cmolik said, "and they are wonderfully appreciated. If you saw one of our customers at the opera, he'd probably stick out like a sore thumb. But they're all hard-working pioneers, and we appreciate them probably more than they think we do. They will always receive a fair and honest deal when they're dealing with Ritchie Bros."[45]

NOTES TO SOURCES

Chapter One

1. Dave Ritchie, interview by Bill Kimmett, tape recording, May 1999, Write Stuff Enterprises.
2. Tammy Ritchie, interview by Jeffrey L. Rodengen, tape recording, June 1999, Write Stuff Enterprises.
3. Bill Ritchie, war service gratuity, Dave Ritchie's personal archives.
4. "Opportunity Knocks for Ritchie Bros.," *Truck Logger,* December/January 1996.
5. Ibid.
6. Dave Ritchie, interview by Jeffrey L. Rodengen, tape recording, 8 August 2000, Write Stuff Enterprises.
7. Bill Bennett, interview by Bill Kimmett, tape recording, 23 August 1999, Write Stuff Enterprises.
8. Dave Ritchie, interview, 8 August 2000.
9. Ibid.
10. Bennett, interview.
11. Dave Ritchie, interview, 8 August 2000.
12. Dave Ritchie, interview, May 1999.
13. Ibid.
14. "Opportunity Knocks."
15. Ken Ritchie, interview by Jeffrey L. Rodengen and Bill Kimmett, tape recording, 21 July 1999, Write Stuff Enterprises.
16. Dave Ritchie, interview, May 1999.
17. Ken Ritchie, interview, 21 July 1999.
18. John Ritchie, interview by Jeffrey L. Rodengen and Bill Kimmett, tape recording, 21 July 1999, Write Stuff Enterprises.

19. Ken Ritchie, interview, 21 July 1999.
20. Schedule "A," Ritchie Bros. Auctioneers, December 1997.
21. Dave Ritchie, interview, May 1999.
22. Ibid.
23. Bennett, interview.
24. John Ritchie, interview.
25. "Opportunity Knocks."
26. "Open for Bids," *McLeans,* 29 May 1978.
27. Ibid.

Chapter Two

1. *Kelowna Capital News,* 30 August 1961.
2. Ken Ritchie, interview, 21 July 1999.
3. "Bringing You a Global Market- place," Ritchie Bros. archives, 8.
4. Ken Ritchie, interview, 21 July 1999.

5. Dave Ritchie, interview by Jon VanZile, tape recording, 17 February 2000, Write Stuff Enterprises.
6. "Opportunity Knocks."
7. Tammy Ritchie, interview by Jeffrey L. Rodengen and Bill Kimmett, tape recording, 22 July 1999, Write Stuff Enterprises.
8. Dick Bartel, interview by Jeff Rodengen and Bill Kimmett, tape recording, 21 July 1999, Write Stuff Enterprises.
9. Peter Van Vreumingen, interview by Bill Kimmett, tape recording, 23 August 1999, Write Stuff Enterprises.
10. Roland Russell, interview by Jon VanZile, tape recording, 8 February 2000, Write Stuff Enterprises.

11. Dave Ritchie, interview, May 1999.
12. Ken Ritchie, interview, 21 July 1999.
13. "Opportunity Knocks,"
14. Van Vreumingen, interview.
15. "Open for Bids," *McLeans,* 1997.
16. Van Vreumingen, interview.
17. Vic Walls, interview by Jon VanZile, tape recording, 14 March 2000, Write Stuff Enterprises.
18. Matt Campbell, interview by Jon VanZile, tape recording, 3 February 2000, Write Stuff Enterprises.
19. Bill Bremmeyer, interview by Jon VanZile, tape recording, 20 December 1999, Write Stuff Enterprises.
20. Ken Ritchie, interview, 21 July 1999.
21. John Reid, interview by Bill Kimmett,

tape recording, 25 August 1999, Write Stuff Enterprises.

22. Dave Ritchie, interview by Jeffrey L. Rodengen, tape recording, 9 August 2000, Write Stuff Enterprises.

23. Ibid.

24. "Open for Bids," 1997.

25. John Wild, interview by Jeffrey L. Rodengen and Bill Kimmett, tape recording, 22 July 1999, Write Stuff Enterprises.

Chapter Three

1. Dave Ritchie, interview, 8 August 2000.

2. Russell, interview.

3. Campbell, interview.

4. Terry Simpson, interview by Jeffrey L. Rodengen, tape recording, 9 February 2000, Write Stuff Enterprises.

5. Frank Forst, interview by Bill

Kimmett, 31 May 1999, Write Stuff Enterprises.

6. Bartel, interview, 21 July 1999.

7. Dave Ritchie, interview, 8 August 2000.

8. Dave Ritchie, interview, 9 August 2000,

9. Ken Ritchie, interview, 21 July 1999.

10. Mike Ritchie, correspondence to Russ Cmolik, 12 June 2000, Ritchie Bros. archives.

11. Dave Ritchie's briefing notes, Dave Ritchie's personal archive.

12. Ibid.

13. Dave Ritchie, interview, 8 August 2000,

14. "Opportunity Knocks."

15. Dave Ritchie, interview, 9 August 2000.

16. Van Vreumingen, interview.

17. Campbell, interview.

18. Russ Cmolik, interview by Jeffrey

L. Rodengen and Bill Kimmett, tape recording, 22 July 1999, Write Stuff Enterprises.

19. Ibid.

Chapter Four

1. Dave Ritchie, interview, 8 August 2000.

2. Ibid.

3. Cmolik, interview, 22 July 1999.

4. John Ritchie, interview.

5. Ibid.

6. Cmolik, interview, 22 July 1999.

7. Ibid.

8. Bob Carswell, interview by Jeffrey L. Rodengen, tape recording, 22 July 1999, Write Stuff Enterprises.

9. Dave Ritchie, interview, 17 February 2000.

10. Cmolik, interview, 22 July 1999.

11. Bartel, interview, 21 July 1999.

12. Cmolik, interview, 22 July 1999.
13. Ken Ritchie, interview by Jeffrey L. Rodengen, tape recording, 22 July 1999, Write Stuff Enterprises.
14. Cmolik, interview, 22 July 1999.
15. Bartel, interview, 21 July 1999.
16. Cmolik, interview, 22 July 1999.
17. Dave Ritchie, interview, 8 August 2000.
18. Ibid.
19. Malcolm Clay, interview by Jon VanZile, tape recording, 24 January 2000, Write Stuff Enterprises.
20. John Ritchie, interview.
21. *Roundup*, 12 July 1977.
22. Cmolik, interview, 22 July 1999.
23. Ibid.
24. *Roundup*, 12 July 1977.
25. Russell, interview.

26. Cmolik, interview, 22 July 1999.
27. Bremmeyer, interview.
28. Simpson, interview.
29. Dick Bartel, interview by Jeffrey L. Rodengen and Bill Kimmett, tape recording, 22 July 1999, Write Stuff Enterprises.
30. *Province*, 25 August 1977.
31. *Roundup*, 12 July 1977.
32. Ibid
33. *Powell River News*, 14 September 1977.
34. Dave Ritchie, interview, 8 August 2000.
35. Frank McFadden, interview by Jeffrey L. Rodengen and Bill Kimmett, tape recording, 22 July 1999, Write Stuff Enterprises.
36. *Supply Post*, June/July 1977.
37. *Financial Post*, 22 October 1977.
38. *Roundup*, 12 July 1977.

39. *Financial Post.*

Chapter Five

1. Carswell, interview.
2. Gary Caufield, interview by Jeffrey L. Rodengen, 22 July 1999, Write Stuff Enterprises.
3. *Purchasing in Western Canada,* December 1977.
4. McFadden, interview.
5. Ibid.
6. Bartel, interview, 22 July 1999.
7. Mike Ritchie, correspondence to Russ Cmolik, 20 June 2000.
8. Tammy Ritchie, interview, 22 July 1999.
9. Caufield, interview.
10. *Roundup*, 1979.
11. Caufield, interview.
12. *Roundup*, 1979.
13. Ibid.

Chapter Six

1. Simpson, interview.
2. Prospectus for Ritchie Bros. Auctioneers.

3. Ibid.

4. Ibid.

5. Ed Banser, interview by Jon VanZile, tape recording, 28 December 1999, Write Stuff Enterprises.

6. Roger Rummel, interview by Jeffrey L. Rodengen, tape recording, 8 February 2000, Write Stuff Enterprises.

7. Randy Ringhaver, interview by Jon VanZile, tape recording, 27 January 2000, Write Stuff Enterprises.

8. Ibid.

9. Ibid.

10. *Roundup*, 1983.

11. Ringhaver, interview.

12. Bob Brawley, interview by Jon VanZile, tape recording, 20 January 2000, Write Stuff Enterprises.

13. John Ivester, interview by Jon VanZile, tape recording, 20 January 2000, Write Stuff Enterprises.

14. *Los Angeles Times*, 24 January 1983.

15. John A. Conway, ed., "Trends," *Forbes*, 29 July 1985, 8.

16. Rick Hullett, interview by Bill Kimmett, tape recording, 2 September 1999, Write Stuff Enterprises.

17. Wild, interview.

18. *Calgary Herald*, 16 May 1980.

19. Dave Ritchie, interview, 8 August 2000.

20. *Calgary Herald*.

21. *National View*, June/July 1985.

22. Bartel, interview, 21 July 1999.

23. Ibid.

24. Don Chalmers, interview by Jon VanZile, tape recording, 19 January 2000, Write Stuff Enterprises.

25. Dave Ritchie, interview, 17 February 2000.

26. *Roundup*, 1986.

27. *Brighton Blade*, 18 May 1986.

Chapter Seven

1. *Port News*, November 1986.

2. Dave Ritchie, interview, 8 August 2000.

3. *Roanoke Times*, 10 April 1987.

4. Bill Miller, interview by Jon VanZile, tape recording, 16 February 2000, Write Stuff Enterprises.

5. Banser, interview.

6. E. R. "Butch" Graham, interview by Jon VanZile, tape recording, 31 August 2000, Write Stuff Enterprises.

7. Dave Kruse, interview by Jon VanZile, tape recording, 20 January 2000, Write Stuff Enterprises.

8. Cmolik, interview, 22 July 1999.

9. Ringhaver, interview.

10. Sylvain Touchette, interview by Jeffrey L. Rodengen, tape recording, 7 February 2000, Write Stuff Enterprises.

11. "Opportunity Knocks."

12. Touchette, interview.

13. *Equipment Journal*, 24 March 1988.

14. *Orlando Business Journal*, 24–30 April 1988.

15. Graham, interview.

16. *Orlando Business Journal*.

17. Kruse, interview.

18. *Equipment Journal*, 24 March 1988.

19. Dave Husby, interview by Bill Kimmett, tape recording, 26 August 1999, Write Stuff Enterprises.

20. *Edmonton Journal*, 26 October 1989.

21. Ibid.

Chapter Eight

1. "Firms Shifting Gears on Equipment," *Engineering News-Record*, 23 March 1992, 34.

2. Banser, interview.

3. *Equipment World*, October 1990.

4. Randy Wall, interview by Jeffrey L. Rodengen, tape recording, 7 September 2000, Write Stuff Enterprises.

5. *Equipment World*.

6. "Auctions: What Am I Bid for the Slick?" *Time*, 22 October 1990, 56.

7. Bartel, interview, 21 July 1999.

8. Larry Stewart, "How to Capitalize on Today's Used-machine Boom," *Construction Equipment*, August 1994, 24.

9. Sheila McGovern, "Heavy Bidding," *Gazette*, 15 April 1995, C3.

10. Ibid.

11. Rob Mackay, interview by Jon VanZile, tape recording, 18 September 2000, Write Stuff Enterprises.

12. Cmolik, interview, 22 July 1999.

13. Russ Cmolik, interview by Jeffrey L. Rodengen, tape recording, 13 July 2000, Write Stuff Enterprises.

14. Ibid.

15. Cmolik, interview, 22 July 1999.

16. Richard Blackwell, "Free-port Status Draws Canadian Firms," *Financial Post*, 6 October 1994, 6.

17. Mackay, interview.

18. Peter Blake, interview by Jon VanZile, tape recording, 5 September 2000, Write Stuff Enterprises.

19. Mackay, interview.

20. "Australia's Largest Auction," *Mining Journal*, 18 April 1997, 307.

21. Mackay, interview.

22. "P.E.I. Bridge Builder to Auction Off Tools," *Toronto Star,* 7 June 1997, E2.

23. Clay Tippett, interview by Jeffrey L. Rodengen and Bill Kimmett, tape recording, 22 July 1999, Write Stuff Enterprises.

24. *Building and Construction News,* April 1999.

25. *Gulf News Business,* 15 October 1997

26. Ibid.

27. Wall, interview.

Chapter Nine

1. Barbara Aarsteinsen, "Ritchie Draws Heavy-duty Customers," *Vancouver Sun,* 21 April 1998, D1.

2. Charles Mandel, "Sale of the New Machine," *Canadian Business,* 13 February 1998, 78.

3. Ibid.

4. McFadden, interview.

5. Ibid.

6. Tippett, interview.

7. Cmolik, interview, 22 July 1999.

8. Ibid.

9. "Ritchie IPO Makes Splash on NYSE," *Vancouver Sun,* 11 March 1998, D1.

10. Ibid.

11. Ibid.

12. Aarsteinsen, "Ritchie Draws Heavy-duty Customers."

13. Drew Hasselback, "Ritchie Hammers Out Winning Auctions Formula," *Financial Post,* 21 August 1998, 17.

14. Cmolik, interview, 22 July 1999.

15. Ibid.

16. Wall, interview.

17. Cmolik, interview, 13 July 2000.

18. David Steinhart, "Wall Street Applauds Ritchie Growth Story," *Financial Post,* 16 April 1998, 46.

19. Hasselback, "Ritchie Hammers Out Winning Auctions Formula."

20. Ringhaver, interview.

21. Ibid.

22. Ibid.

23. Cmolik, interview, 22 July 1999.

24. Ibid.

25. Ringhaver, interview.

26. Cmolik, interview, 22 July 1999.

27. "Ritchie Bros. Announces New Global Initiatives," Canadian Corporate Newswire, 21 September 1999.

28. *Construction Equipment Guide,* 4 August 1999.

29. *Equipment Journal,* 5 February 1998.

30. Blake, interview.

31. Ritchie Bros. Auctioneers news release, March 2000, Ritchie Bros. corporate archive.

32. Banser, interview.

33. Ivester, interview.

34. Bob Armstrong, interview by Jeffrey L. Rodengen, tape recording, 8 July

2002, Write Stuff Enterprises.

35. Ibid.

36. Bob Leavy, interview by Jeffrey L. Rodengen, tape recording, 8 July 2002, Write Stuff Enterprises.

37. Peter Blake, interview by Jeffrey L. Rodengen, tape recording, 7 June 2002, Write Stuff Enteprises.

38. Stephen Branch, interview by Jeffrey L. Rodengen, tape recording, 13 August 2002, Write Stuff Enterprises.

39. Ibid.

40. Nick Nicholson, interview by Jon VanZile, tape recording, 19 July 2002, Write Stuff Enterprises.

41. Don Breen, interview by Jeffrey L. Rodengen, tape recording, 12 September 2002, Write Stuff Enterprises.

42. Russ Cmolik, interview by Jeffrey L. Rodengen, tape recording, 11 June 2002, Write Stuff Entperprises.

43. Ibid.

44. Chalmers, interview.

45. Cmolik, interview, 22 July 1999.

INDEX